THE RIGHT WAY TO
IMPROVE YOUR MEMORY

GW00507473

By the same author

The Knot Book
Teach Your Child To Swim

Also available from Elliot Right Way Books

THE RIGHT WAY TO IMPROVE YOUR MEMORY

Geoffrey Budworth

RIGHT WAY

"It is all right for beasts to have no memories; but we poor humans must be compensated."

William Bolitho (1891–1930)

ACKNOWLEDGEMENTS

I acknowledge the generosity of A. P. Watt Ltd., literary agents, on behalf of Crystal Hale and Jocelyn Herbert, for granting me permission to include, free of charge, in this book extracts from the late Sir A. P. Herbert's poem *The Bowline*.

I also acknowledge the kind co-operation of Mrs. Pamela Flowers, Mr. Natheer George and Mrs. Jan Grimsley, with whom I once worked, for giving me permission to tell an anecdote concerning each one of them.

CONTENTS

PREAMBLE

"The human memory can be compared to a complex and capacious but untidy filing cabinet."

Cyrus Lawrence DAY (1967)

Beginning

Your memory, which you may consider to be poor, is really quite excellent. It is just that at present you do not have full control of it. So it works haphazardly, and it is this hit-or-miss nature that you can correct.

I expect you can recall scenes from your childhood; you know numerous song lyrics more or less word perfect; you can enjoy a good story, book or film. Your memory is therefore in working order. When you forget (or, more likely, fail to memorise in the first place) the name of a person to whom you have recently been introduced, or where you put things, that is simply because you do not file the facts away properly in your mind. If study is tedious and a waste of time, since little or nothing sinks in, then you are merely going about it the wrong way.

A good memory is NOT a gift. It is a reward. Use it the right way and it will amply repay you.

Short & Long-Term Memory

Learn at once the difference between a short and a long-term memory. Your "short-term" memory is extraordinary. It stores what I say to you, so that, when I finally come to the end of a long-ish sentence (like this one), it makes sense because you can still remember the beginning. You may not have realised that such a process was necessary, but it is, and you use it subconsciously all the time.

When a school teacher challenges an inattentive pupil with; "You, there! What did I say?" the intended victim often turns the tables by repeating word-for-word what has gone before, although in fact he was *not* listening. His short-term memory, like a tape-recorded playback, comes to his rescue.

Mind you, short-term memories have very limited life-spans. What that teacher should have done was waited awhile. As a lecturer I do this myself, then later in the lesson say; "By the way, so-and-so, what did I tell you *earlier* about . . . ?" By then the unheedful student has lost whatever was said. It has been erased or overlaid by later stuff, and not stored in his long-term memory.

Real remembering therefore involves being alert to recognise information you will need again, and, somehow or other, lifting it out of your short-term memory to file it sensibly in your long-term memory. Then you can readily retrieve it hours, days, weeks, months, years or even decades later. That is what this book is mostly about.

Tidying a Wardrobe

Think of when you last tidied your cluttered shed or garage, an over-filled wardrobe, a chaotic filing cabinet, or whatever it might have been. Imagine a bedroom wardrobe, so full there is no room for another item, so disorganised that you cannot find a thing. When you open a door the contents spill out, but they will not fit back in so that you can close the door again. It is time for a sort-out. How do you go about it? We all – I guess – have similar routines. First we empty everything out, dozens of bits and pieces higgledy-piggledy, and spread them around to see what we have. We assess the available storage space. Then we start to put it all away again.

Many items obviously belong in certain places. Jackets and trousers, dresses and skirts, will go on hangers suspended from the rail provided. Shoes go underneath.

Given a nest of drawers, we put small things in the shallow top drawer, e.g. handkerchieves, make-up, ties (unless there is a tie rack), cuff-links and belts. The next drawer down takes larger lightweight garments such as blouses or shirts and underwear. The bottom drawer is usually deeper and into this go chunky woollen sweaters and other bulky clothing.

Then we are left with awkward objects, the placing of which requires decisions. A tennis racquet or a bag of golf clubs can stand behind clothing in the hanging space. That choice almost makes itself, as it is the only volume big enough for them. But what about a hair-dryer, a money belt, that black hat you are keeping for a funeral, a spare pack of cards, the birthday present that must be kept concealed until the right date? We might all differ over precisely where we put each one of these, but eventually everything will be replaced neatly and tidily, accessible, with a place for everything, and everything in this or that place.

Now picture a scene 6 months later. You are downstairs on the living room sofa, immobilised with a broken leg in plaster. A friend calls round and suggests a game of cards. You say; "Pop up to my bedroom. Go to the wardrobe. In the lefthand side, third drawer down, at the back on the right under a blue woolly cardigan, you'll find a new pack there."

Hey, hold on a minute. How do you know after 6 months where you put those cards? I mean, what you actually did when you tidied up was to memorise a long list of personal possessions and a matching list of individual locations. Now, half a year later, you can recall it all perfectly. Isn't that incredible? Well, not really. It is a common experience. We can all do it. But it is pretty impressive, nonetheless. You absorbed those lists effortlessly, without written notes, imprinting them so indelibly on your mind that you can recall any bit of them after a long lapse of time.

So what does that imply?

If we can identify exactly how you did that, so as to do it whenever you choose, perhaps YOU NEED NEVER WORK HARD TO LEARN ANYTHING EVER AGAIN.

LESSON 1
6 GUIDING PRINCIPLES

"Mind power is a trick. And you can learn that trick."
Harry LORAYNE (1961)

Exercise

Try this exercise. Look at the 12 words listed below (counting 2-word items as single entries) and allow yourself just 2 minutes to memorise them all *in the order they occur*.

> GUN
>
> SOME REEL
>
> PLY
>
> APOSTLES
>
> STROKE
>
> WAY
>
> PLUS
>
> SISTERS
>
> CARD TRICK
>
> PINS
>
> FINGER
>
> TOES

DO NOT LOOK AT THE NEXT PAGE
until you have tried this assignment.

Now without referring back to the previous page, answer all of the following if you can.

(a)   Recite the list *backwards* from memory.
(b)   Which was the third word up from the bottom of the list?
(c)   Which word appeared after 'APOSTLES'?
(d)   Name the eleventh word.
(e)   Which word came before 'CARD TRICK'?
(f)   Name every alternate word, starting with 'SOME REEL'.

That was a hard test. How did you cope? Not well, I dare say. Turn back and read again the difficult batch of mostly senseless words I deliberately picked for you to learn. Several could be nouns or verbs, making it hard to picture them in your mind's eye. 'PLUS' is a preposition. And what on earth does 'SOME REEL' refer to? Individuals who have drunk too much alcohol? Or anglers winding in their lines? The list does not tell a story; nor can the initial letters of the 12 items be easily made to spell a code word. As it stands, there is no rhyme or reason to it.

Learning the list in a straightforward way from beginning to end was awkward enough. If you remembered 8 out of 12, that was quick and clever of you. It did not help, however, to answer my questions. To do that you had to know the numerical order of the words so that you could skip from item to item, backwards or forwards, without hesitation. A tall order. No. Look once more at the list. Now you have time to think about it 'CARD TRICK' might remind you of the "*Three* Card Trick (Find the Lady)" performed by shady tricksters and gamblers to separate gullible punters from their cash. Similarly, there are "*Seven* SISTERS", those white cliffs to the West of Beachy Head lighthouse; or, alternatively, the bright stars known as the Pleiades which form an open cluster visible to the naked eye in the constellation of Taurus. Then again, there are "*Twelve* APOSTLES", Christ's 12 disciples. In fact every item in the list can be associated with a different number between 1 and 12. See how they can now be rearranged.

1.	WAY	As in 'One-way street'.
2.	PLY	Like 'Two-ply wool'.
3.	CARD TRICK	'Three card trick'.
4.	STROKE	'Four-stroke engine'.
5.	FINGER...........	'Five finger (piano) exercise'.
6.	GUN...............	'Six-gun (Colt 45 revolver)'.
7.	SISTERS	'Seven Sisters'.
8.	SOME REEL	'Eightsome reel (Scottish dance)'.
9.	PINS	'Ninepins (skittles)'.
10.	TOES	'Ten toes (on one's feet)'.
11.	PLUS	'Eleven-plus examination'.
12.	APOSTLES	'Twelve apostles'.

Please do not think I have tricked you by making you try to learn one list, then changing the order for no good reason. That would be unfair. There is a crucial point to be made by showing you two different lists. It is that memory improves remarkably if you can spot a pattern and sort out whatever must be learnt into a better arrangement. Time and effort devoted to that end is not wasted. Learning is quicker and surer as a consequence.

Now, take your time and learn this new list which, with its numbers, makes a lot more sense. Try to recite the rewritten list from memory, items 1 to 12. If you become stuck for a word, do not worry. Leave it and go on to the others. If it still escapes you, look it up and then try again. When you can recall the entire list, tackle those earlier questions of mine in relation to the revised list. They make you think, but now you can deal with them.

See how your memory improves? Yet your brain is the same. It was the systematic way you applied it that did the trick.

Try some more questions. What *number* in the list is 'TOES'? 'GUN'? 'PLUS'? 'WAY'? You see? You can do it in reverse. Number and word are linked together in your mind. Think of one and you think of the other.

Grasp this valuable concept. Memory improves remarkably when you devote time to making sense of what must be learnt. Do not waste your time trying in vain to memorise material any old how. Actors and actresses do not learn lines by mindless repetition. They first find out the story-line and how their characters are involved in it. Thus the speeches and chat they must deliver make sense, as the words of the other performers on stage serve as cues to prompt their responses.

The similarities between what we did sorting out that cluttered wardrobe and how you came to grips with the list of words are so clearcut that I can highlight for you the features common to both tasks. They are my 6 guiding principles for improving your memory.

---

6 GUIDING PRINCIPLES
(Codeword — M.E.M.O.R.Y.)

1.	M –INUTES, not seconds	allow adequate time
2.	E – VALUATE	take careful stock
3.	M –AKE AN EFFORT	be actively involved
4.	O – RDER THE DATA	rearrange it to make sense
5.	R – EINFORCE	review and repeatedly use
	CURIOSIT	
6.	Y –	become intrigued

NOTES

(i)   Allow adequate time (M-inutes, not seconds)

When you embark upon a bout of Spring-cleaning you set aside as long as necessary. I let you take your own time learning that sorted-out second list of words.

(ii)   Take careful stock (E-valuate)

The indispensable first step to tidying our imaginary wardrobe was spreading everything out, sizing it all up and deciding how to go about putting it back, before we did anything else. Without that forethought we would not have achieved what we did. I gave you no chance to assess the first word list and so it was unmanageable.

(iii)   Be actively involved (M-ake an effort)

Use these principles and it is easy to become involved in the job to hand. Once you realised the word list could be sorted out into a better order, I am sure you thought; "Ah, that's easier. Right. Let's get at it."

(iv)   Rearrange it to make sense (O-rder the data)

You put things back into the wardrobe in a way that made sense to you. Although I rearranged the word list, you could follow my logic. Indeed, after a couple of clues, you could have done it yourself.

(v)   Review and repeatedly use (R-einforce)

Memory is more firmly impressed by repetition. Each succeeding question of mine that you answered increased your grasp of the rearranged list.

(vi)   Become intrigued (Curiosit - y)

Treat study as a puzzle or game. Turn dull and dreary

material into simpler, lively stuff. Simplify anything difficult. Then you can enjoy mastering it.

The experimental word list demonstrated how good your memory is when you allow it to work the way it likes best. The words you learnt are, of course, valueless. The sooner you forget them the better. So we will not refer to, or use, them again.

My 6 guiding principles are, on the other hand, indispensable. That is why I contrived the code word M.E.M.O.R.Y. to help you picture them; and why I also repeated each one of the headings, and enlarged a little upon them, in the notes (i) to (vi). We will reinforce them in later lessons.

LESSON 2
SOME RUDIMENTS

"Everyone complains of his memory . . ."
                    Duc De La Rochefoucauld (1613–1680)

Fahrenheit 451

In his classic science fiction novel *Fahrenheit 451* published in 1953 American author Ray Bradbury describes a future society in which all books are burnt, to prevent them influencing and unsettling the largely submissive citizenry. The title refers to the temperature at which paper burns. Most people in this fantastic tale (later made into a film by French director Francois Truffaut) accept that it is for their own good, and even inform on neighbours who dare to own and read books in secret. Dissidents can only flee. The story ends where a refugees' colony forms at a safe distance from the authorities, a colony where every adult "is a book"; that is, he or she has committed an entire written book to memory, word-for-word. One man is the *Book of Ecclesiastes*, another Plato's *Republic*, a third Jonathan Swift's *Gulliver's Travels*, while a group represents the complete *Essays* of Bertrand Russell. Others have learnt texts from writers as diverse as Marcus Aurelius (the Roman Stoic 'Philosopher-Emperor'), British Victorian novelist Charles Dickens and the German philosopher Arthur Schopenhauer. Einstein, Confucius, Thomas Jefferson (who drafted the American *Declaration of Independence*), and the biblical New Testament gospellers Matthew, Mark, Luke and John, all are preserved. Each one of these rare individuals is duty bound to recite his tale to anyone wishing to hear it, and also to pass it on to one of the next generation.

No mean memory feat. But, before the written word was widespread, races of people did rely entirely upon just such story-tellers and wise men to preserve and pass on their history and heritage. These professional narrators developed extraordinary memories, devising aids to remembering that we still use today. Some appear in this book.

Simonides & William Woodfall

The celebrated Ancient Greek poet Simonides lived from about 556 to 468 B.C. Although he is reported to have been of unattractive appearance, he was an excellent business man and became the first Greek poet to profit greatly from his writing and performing. Possibly the earliest – and surely the most dramatic – account of a trained memory at work involved him. About 500 B.C., shortly after he left a banquet where he had entertained the Scopades, rulers of Thessaly, the palace collapsed burying the host, his family and guests. Because we today have seen film newsreels of the aftermath of earthquakes, bombs and similar disasters, we can picture the chaos. Those digging in the rubble for possible survivors did not know exactly where to look, or how many there might be. Some of the bodies they did find were disfigured beyond recognition. Simonides, using skills that had won him 56 poetical contests, summoned up a mental picture of how the seating layout had been earlier, when he was there, and, so (the legend goes), was able to locate, identify and name all the victims.

In 1789, during George III's reign, William 'Memory' Woodfall (1746–1803) established a journal entitled *The Diary*, which became the first such paper able to report Parliamentary proceedings the morning after their occurrence. He would attend the debates and then, without notes and demonstrating a capacity for vivid recall, report them accurately.

Those two historical characters are obviously supreme examples of how memory can be made to serve usefully. Understand however, that many people in those times habitually made the effort to memorise information. They relied less than we do upon the written or printed word. We are often lost without a memo pad, diary or bulky 'personal organiser'. Now a personal organiser is an excellent product . . . but we buy them, I suspect, because the marketing folk have sold us that it is smart and essential. The truth is we probably use only a small fraction of the contents and could do as well if we exercised our brains a little more.

Animals and Humankind

"I have a memory like an elephant. In fact elephants often consult me", witty and worldly British dramatist, composer and entertainer Sir Noel Coward is quoted as saying to U.S. ambassador and Harvard professor John Kenneth Galbraith. The notion that elephants never forget is a persistent one. Sadly, this may be a travellers' tall tale, akin to reports of the Indian rope trick. Everyone has an anecdote about it. Nobody has actually witnessed the evidence at first hand.

In fact, animal behaviourists doubt that memory plays much of a part in how animals perform. Do our pets really understand every word we say? Does a returning salmon "remember" the taste of its home river from the time as a silvery smolt it migrated to the sea? It is more likely, according to our present knowledge, that animal behaviour is stimulated by the needs of the moment. They survive on innate skills and a quickness to meet challenges, rather than from recalling past events or planning for the future. What it boils down to is that they may simply be very, very alert to spot tell-tale favourable signs, enabling them to learn by trial without much error, and so behave in ways that bring prompt rewards.

Indeed, so-called "dumb animals" can be better than humankind in some circumstances, by *not* relying upon memory. Few human beings can build a house without first serving a lengthy apprenticeship. Then it takes a team including architects, planners, bricklayers, carpenters, plumbers and electricians, to complete the project. A bird or animal that has never seen another of its own kind build a nest or lair may still make an excellent job of one itself when it feels the urge to do so. Creatures rely upon fixed action patterns, triggered by the right stimulus to respond at the proper time. This saves a lot of learning but it has its limitations. They are slaves to instinct and cannot readily adapt. A female rabbit plucking fur from her breast and urgently making a nest when she is not pregnant is a sight you may view as comic or sad. It is wholly inappropriate behaviour.

Humankind seems to be separated from animals by memory. In developing and relying upon memory we gave up reflex action in favour of acquired learning. Thus far it has enabled us to survive and evolve.

It is assumed that 400,000 years ago upright man (Homo Erectus), the first human, had some kind of memory because he probably had crude speech, and there is evidence of planned hunting and social organisation. Again, 200,000 years later, Neanderthal man practised simple art and ritual. He also buried his dead with gifts, goods and clothing. That suggests belief in an afterlife, while the poignant find of a posy of flowers by a graveside could imply a capacity to mourn.

Forget-Me-Knots

One of mankind's earliest memory aids was knots, the sort tied in string and rope. Early men used knots for hunting, fishing and hauling loads, even for First Aid or rough-and-ready surgery. Knots pre-date fire, the wheel, cultivation of the soil and harnessing the wind. Stone Age men tied knots, as much of what they made was wood lashed together with flexible reeds, vines or rawhide strips. They also used them for religious and magical purposes, to pass on history and culture, and as simple but effective memory aids.

Say that you and I are tribal chiefs meeting at intervals to discuss our mutual safety and survival. Before we part we must arrange our next monthly get-together. We cannot write. Anyway there is no postal service. We live too far apart for smoke signals or beacon fires. Also we shall be travelling, on the move where no messenger on foot or horseback could be sure to locate us. What can we do? Well, I have a length of twine or cord tied with 30 knots and I give you an identical one. I say to you; "Take this cord and each time the sun rises untie one knot. I will do the same. When the last knots have gone, then we shall meet here again." Simple. That is what many ancient peoples did . . . and were still doing early this century. Ancient Greeks, Africans, American Indians, Solomon Islanders, and many others, tied such knot calendars or diaries. Perhaps tying a knot around one's finger or in one's handkerchief, to remember something, came about this way.

The late Sir Alan P. Herbert (1890–1971) was a playwright, lyricist, author and wit, and M.P. for Oxford University (when the University had its very own M.P.). He was an experienced sailor who during World War II put himself and his motor launch at the Nation's disposal, patrolling the Pool of London down to the lower reaches of the Thames Estuary, mine-spotting, fire-watching, securing drifting barges and undertaking other waterman's work. He became a confidant of river policemen, bargemen and lightermen. Sir Alan wrote a poem in praise of knots. It was called *The Bowline* and a part of it says;

". . . at the earliest wife's remark
'Again you have forgot'
the earliest husband's handkerchief
received this noble knot."

That could go wrong. Imagine. An old man sits dozing at a table outside a Continental café. His large handkerchief hangs loosely from a pocket. A mischievous young man, taking care not to disturb the old chap, ties a knot in it. When the oldster finally awakes and tidies himself to leave, he finds the knot – and spends the remainder of the day fretting at forgetting whatever it was he wrongly supposes he must have wanted to recall.

The Ancient Hebrews seem to have used knotted cords or fringes to pass on, or at least to symbolise, traditions and codes of law. It is only a small step from this to the rosary of knots or beads used in the recitation by some of prayers, or of the names of gods. The 3 knots in the waist-tie worn by nuns and monks remind them of their vows of poverty, chastity and obedience. They are thus bound to their vocation, tied to their celibacy. Much of the regalia and insignia, including lanyards and sashes, worn by military and civil dignitaries today, symbolically binds the wearers to their rôles, reminds them of their duties. Heraldry too, depicting the factors associated with the fortunes of family or city, features several heraldic knots.

Memory systems were certainly taught from the 12th century, and many races kept detailed accounts of their possessions, cattle, grain harvests, census statistics, tax details, and all kinds of things, by means of coloured and knotted cords. The most well-known are the *quipus* of the Peruvian Incas that can be seen and studied in museums around the world. They were superseded by the abacus, that handy counting arrangement of rods and sliding beads on a frame. Some scholars believe the abacus may have developed from knotted cords.

The game of Cat's Cradle, played by European children, consists of a few comparatively simple interlaced patterns in string that is passed from hand to hand. Little or no attempt is made to weave a story with the string. Earlier peoples made a more elaborate game of it. From Alaska to Zanzibar, Angola to New Zealand, in Japan and Peru and the Gilbert Islands, the string figures they created were closely connected with their racial histories and mythology. Traditional tales were told, illustrated by string outlines with names like *Fighting Headhunters*, *Fish Spear*, *Rattlesnake and a Boy*, a *Palm Tree*, a *Canoe with Two Masts*, *Apache Teepee*, etc. They were a part of the folk lore.

Mighty Memory

Brought up to read and write and now type into some data processing set-up, we under-estimate the power of our memories. Consider. Your memory is truly capacious. Try to think of all you know, everything you can recollect. There is, for a start, the accumulation of all that has occurred to you, directly or indirectly, throughout your unique lifetime: then what you know from reading and hearing about other people's experiences. You will also have knowledge, real or wrong (but it is stored anyway and is there to be recalled), about the wide world in general. It seems never-ending as you attempt to dredge it all up. You never reach the bottom. The capacity of your memory is vast, while the speed of recall (recognition and retrieval without first scanning the whole lot) can be awesome.

The Goblin Syndrome

Short-term memory has a limited capacity. It may be, however, that ALL information has to pass through it on its way to long-term storage. So a methodical approach to study is essential if short-term memory is not to be temporarily overloaded and fail you – the Goblin Syndrome.

You must at some time have mislaid an object; been unable to find it again despite a prolonged search; and all the time insisted you knew nothing of its whereabouts. I know I have. We deny all knowledge of the missing item, accuse everyone else of taking it, or else resign ourselves to the fact that it has somehow disappeared into thin air never to be seen again. "There's a goblin in this house," we say. "Nothing's safe. You can't leave anything lying around. It just disappears."

Later, when it comes to light in some odd place we had not thought to look, we remember – shamefacedly – that we did put it there. It had slipped our memory. I actually caught myself the other day putting a nautical chart of Poole Harbour into a box file labelled 'Income Tax Returns' instead of the one marked 'Canoeing'.

The Goblin Syndrome occurs from total neglect of my 6 guiding principles. Here is a scenario. I am trying to complete several important tasks at once. Time is against me. Suddenly the thought pops into my mind that an overdue library book has to be returned. With only a bit of my mind on it, I reach out a hand and pick up the book to put it somewhere I will see it next time I go out in the direction of the library. At that moment the doorbell rings. "Dash it! Am I to have no peace?" I exclaim. More preoccupied with how unfairly the world is treating me than what I am doing, I answer the door. It is the milkman to be paid. I go in search of my wife's housekeeping money. Along the way, absentmindedly, I dump the book so as to have my hands free. After paying the milkman I go back to where I left off. The library book is forgotten, on top of the fridge, in the cloakroom with the wellington boots and a vacuum cleaner, anywhere but where you would think to look for it. As far as I am now concerned, the incident with the book might never have happened. It is out of sight and out of mind. That is the Goblin Syndrome.

Look again at the 6 guiding principles.

1.	**M** – INUTES, not seconds	I gave no time to thinking where I put that library book.
2.	**E** – valuate..................	I exercised no foresight.
3.	**M** – ake an Effort	I was actively involved in paying the milkman but I discarded the book without any consideration at all.
4.	**O** – rder the data	I put the book where it made no sense.
5.	**R** – einforce	I did not give it another thought.
6.	Curiosit – **Y**	My interest was in other matters.

The Goblin Syndrome only occurs when the 6 guiding principles are disregarded, so we can take steps to avoid it in future.

Use, or Lose

Some psychologists claim no experience is ever forgotten; that our sub-conscious harbours memories beyond recall that could be retrieved by experts. Memory is thought to be mainly a chemical process, although initial data collection via our 5 senses seems also to involve electrical activity. For everyday purposes, however, it seems that memory – like a computer programmed to erase data after a certain length of time – allows some unused knowledge to become extinct. This periodic tidy of the mental attic is not properly understood. It may be more likely to happen with recently acquired facts. When we study for an examination, then pour it all out on exam day into written answers on paper, a few weeks or months later we have forgotten much of it. Fair enough. We may not have used or reinforced it since. What you do not use, you may lose.

Men and women with trained memories are still capable of lapses that make their friends chortle. I demonstrate memory training techniques to students in the classroom. If I take a textbook on the subject into class with me, I often leave it there by mistake. Sooner or later there is a knock on the door, followed by a gleeful; "Excuse me, Sir. Here's your memory-training book. You've forgotten it again."

Me, For Example

My schooling was disrupted when we moved, my parents and I, from Oakham (county town of Rutland, then England's smallest county) to Bournemouth on the South coast in Hampshire. My early home town geography is now out-of-date, by the way, re-drawn by the local government reorganisation of the early 1970s. I was 8 and had, until then, done well in our small market town primary school. The school at Bournemouth had a curriculum a year ahead of what I had been doing. I never caught up. I failed my 11+ exam. Although still selected to go to the grammar school, I barely coped there from year to year in the bottom stream. I was convinced I was no scholar, set myself low standards, and fell in with a lot of dunderheads. The teachers no doubt saw little potential in me.

After leaving school I survived in the workplace because it made a lot more sense to me. By a happy chance I joined the Metropolitan Police Cadet Corps. Then, after 2 years away on compulsory National Service in the Army, I became a probationer beat constable in London's West End. It was 1956.

Recruit training was intensive and thorough. Detailed book work included criminal law, and Force procedures. Whether or not there is a comma in some legal definition can make a vital difference to its interpretation in a court trial, so even the rawest beginner had to be strictly schooled. I did well, surprisingly, holding my own with better academically qualified mates.

It takes 2 years to qualify as a constable, a time punctuated by returns to the classroom and further examinations. Promotion is then, not by spectacular arrests, but by the sheer grind of study for very stiff competitive exams. The first 5 to 10 years of an ambitious copper's life are taken up with theory study. If you are not a student to start with, you must quickly become one.

I was in Thames Division – London's River Police – and a constable with about 5 years' service when I began to collect and use odd tricks and devices calculated to improve my memory. It was a turning point. No longer did I merely pass tests. Sometimes I excelled. Soon I accepted this as normal. I grew more confident. When occasionally I did not do so well, I knew it was due only to lack of application and that it could be rectified.

I went on to serve 3 tours of duty totalling 7 years as an instructor at the prestigious Hendon Training School and become a member of the probationers' examination panel. When I left the Police, aged 44 as an Inspector with 25 years' service, to start a second career, it was baths & leisure management that attracted me.

This meant taking a job as a swimming pool lifeguard and learning the job from the poolside up, a scrubbing brush in one hand and my other arm down a blocked-up toilet. I undertook a 3 year correspondence course in local government administration, personnel management, the operation of recreational facilities, and water treatment & engineering. This was topped-up with day-release for a year at South East London College, where I was in a class with youngsters who were half my age and had had longer in the industry than I. A few were university graduates.

When I took the Membership examination of the Institute of Bath & Recreation Managers, I passed out top U.K. examinee.

The following year I was top U.K. examinee once again, this time in the I.B.R.M.'s Diploma examination.

Those were sweet moments for a lad who once thought he was no scholar, and proof of the effectiveness of memory-training techniques combined with a systematic approach to study. All I knew and used then to do with memory is here in this book.

LESSON 3
ASSOCIATION OF IDEAS

"Ah, that reminds me . . ."

(Trad.)

'007' – Licensed to Kill

"I'm stuck," said one of my assistant managers. "I can't complete this form the Personnel Department wants without fail today, because I don't have old what's-'is-name's pay code, and he's off sick until further notice."

"No problem," I replied. "It's 007."

You can imagine how your reputation at work is enhanced by incidents like that ("The guv'nor's amazing; knows everyone's pay codes!"). I don't really. That particular one stuck in my memory for a funny reason. The owner of the number had a reputation for stirring up grievances in others but was careful never to be caught grumbling himself. He "made bullets for others to fire", as the saying goes. So, when I first heard that his pay code was '007', it tickled my imagination. How apt, I thought. Ian Fleming's fictional character James Bond, quick-on-the-trigger (a mental association with "bullets") and licensed to kill, is also known as '007'.

This association of ideas occurred to me quicker than I can write it down here (as quick as thought, literally) yet, as a consequence, I can recall those figures without effort whenever his name is mentioned. Conversely, tell me the number and I can put the right name to it. That is the useful thing about using an association of ideas. The mental link works just as well either way, as you discovered with that word list in Lesson 1.

Yo-yos

A children's entertainer, a clown, whom I meet regularly at a magic society uses yo-yos in his act. When he heard that I collect antique ones, he asked me to bring some along for him to see.

"I'll bring them to the next meeting," I promised.

I made a mental note to do so (wrote nothing down) and did not give it another thought until I was getting ready to go out to that meeting a month later, when the thought 'I must take those yo-yos' came into my head.

How was it done? Easily. I knew I would have to go to my den to pick up one or two conjuring bits-&-pieces before the next meeting. I always do. So, while still speaking with him, I just pictured myself collecting that paraphernalia and some yo-yos at the same time. The knack is to pick and picture a place where you will certainly be at the moment you must think once more about the yo-yos, or whatever it is.

Why not simply use a diary or write yourself a note? That would be okay if you could rely upon seeing it again at the right moment. But it is not foolproof. You might mislay it – beware of the Goblin Syndrome (Lesson 2) – or put the note somewhere so secure, like a rarely used inner pocket of your wallet, that it does not see light of day for a year. A mental association of ideas is actually more reliable. Concentrate upon your chosen image for a few seconds. Do not let your mind wander. Then let it go. When you need it, it will come to you.

We are continually let down by people who fail to keep their promises, and become resigned to the fact that messages will not be passed on, phone calls will not be returned. How refreshing it is when we deal with someone who does remember obligations unprompted. Naturally we give them our business and our friendship. Now you know how to do it.

Months of the Year

Suppose you have, in rough order for carrying them out, the following dozen jobs to do tomorrow:-

1. Take a reference book from your home to work where you need it.

2. Visit the post office to buy eight 1st class stamps.

3. Complete an annual leave application form and submit it to your departmental head.

4. Visit the optician in your lunch hour.

5. Renew your season ticket at the local swimming pool.

6. Buy a jar of coffee and a box of tea bags for the office tea club.

7. Make appointments to see 2 probationer employees to discuss their progress.

8. Compile annual statistics and forward them to the company's finance department.

9. Return a telephone call.

10. Look closely at your street atlas before leaving work for home, to see if you can find an alternative route that avoids an awkward right turn across a busy main road.

11. Collect the cat from the vet.

12. Reset your alarm clock for an early start the following day.

This job list cannot conveniently be rearranged to make better sense; but, to memorise no more than 12 items at a time, you can use another mnemonic link. (Regarding mnemonics see also Lesson 4.) Which 12 nouns do we also represent by numbers, so often, that we use the words and numbers interchangeably? The months of the year. Anyone writing a date on a letter, or beside his signature on a form, has to decide whether to write the word for the month or to substitute its number:-

1.	JANUARY	7.	JULY
2.	FEBRUARY	8.	AUGUST
3.	MARCH	9.	SEPTEMBER
4.	APRIL	10.	OCTOBER
5.	MAY	11.	NOVEMBER
6.	JUNE	12.	DECEMBER

You know that March is 3, August is 8, 10 is October, and so on, almost without thinking. If you settle on a distinct mental picture of each month, then, by linking these pictures with the items you want to remember, you can keep them in strict numerical order too.

I have a clear mental image for each month. I will tell you what they are, but they are personal and may be of no use to you. You must make your own. Mine are:-

1. **JANUARY** is the start of the New Year, so I picture the traditional scenes of celebration I have witnessed often around the statue of Eros in London's Piccadilly Circus. Anything I need to remember first on a short list I put somehow into this scene.

2. **FEBRUARY** is my birthday month. I pretend I am at a party, opening my presents. One of them is item number two on the list.

3. **MARCH** is the month when my elder daughter was born. I do not use another birthday. That would only confuse me. I just link the 3rd thing on the list with an image of her.

4. APRIL   is often a showery month. No. 4 on the
                 list I drench with April showers.

5. MAY   "April showers bring forth May
                 flowers." I set the 5th object amongst
                 such flowers.

6. JUNE   is the month I was married, so I use
                 the scenery outside the Warwickshire
                 village church as my background for
                 item No. 6. (You might think of
                 "flaming June" with sunny blue sky.)

7. JULY   I once did a July end-of-term school
                 study project about Shakespeare's play
                 Julius Caesar, so Julius is my link with
                 No. 7 on the list.

8. AUGUST   Working in the leisure industry, as I
                 do, this month brings to my mind
                 school holidays when swimming pools
                 and leisure centres are inundated by
                 children and young people. I fit the
                 8th task on the list into such a scene.

9. SEPTEM-   My younger daughter was born in this
    BER   month, so she is my picture.

10. OCTOBER   I use an image of the Russian
                 Revolution, because Lenin's
                 Bolsheviks seized control of the central
                 organs of power on Oct 25 (old style
                 calendar).

11. NOVEM-   I remember London's "pea-souper"
    BER   fogs, when you could barely see your
                 hand in front of your face, and you
                 really could become lost in an area you
                 knew well. Rightly or wrongly, I think
                 of these happening in November.

12.	DECEM- BER	Christmas. I call to mind a typical Dickensian festive picture with Yule log fire, snow outside, and people full of pudding, jollity and goodwill.

Here is how I would memorise, in a few minutes, using no notes, that day's list of errands and jobs I gave earlier.

1. I am coming downstairs at home on my way to breakfast (because I am one who would not miss breakfast for anything). Eros confronts me, blocking my way at the foot of the stairway. He is waving in front of my eyes, reprovingly, the book I must take with me. That cannot fail. I go and get it, putting it into my briefcase, before I forget!

2. My elaborately gift-wrapped birthday present, when I open it to the applause and congratulations of all my relatives and friends, is . . . eight first class postage stamps. (Absurd, isn't it? But it works.)

   Incidentally, I ask myself 'What is No. 2 on today's list?' just as soon as I have recalled and carried out No. 1 (that library book), so as not to miss any deadline.

3. My elder daughter is struggling to hold aloft a giant leave application form. It is several sizes larger than her. She is saying to me; 'You'll need this, Dad."

4. I am out in torrential rain. It streams down my spectacles, blurring my vision. I cannot see. I must go to the optician.

5. There is a bank of flowers; better, a field of flowers, or a world of giant flowers, into which I plunge head-first to swim crawl stroke. That reminds me, I must renew my season ticket at the swimming pool.

6. Posing for my wedding photograph in the churchyard after the service, I am laden with armfuls of coffee jars and boxes of tea bags. They spill over to land on the

ground. The vicar is annoyed by the mess. The photographer is cross at the distraction and delay. The guests are staring at me. All I know is that I must buy more tea and coffee.

7.   Julius Caesar, in robes and laurel wreath, sits at my office desk interrogating my 2 probationers. I must do that, I remember.

8.   As it is my business, picturing the Summer holiday action at a pool or leisure centre is bound to trigger off thoughts in my mind of attendance and income figures. A statistical return is indicated.

9.   I recall my younger daughter, when she was a very little girl, playing with a toy plastic telephone. That reminds me, I must return a call of my own.

10.   I am a driver of a horse-drawn carriage laden with individuals who are fleeing the 'October Revolution'. We need an escape route that avoids the Bolshevik revolutionaries. I must look up that car route on the map.

11.   I am wandering, hopelessly lost, in a London fog. For some reason I have with me my cat in her carrying-basket. Of course, I am bringing her back from the vet.

12.   An early awakening is unavoidable on Christmas Day, with youngsters up-and-about eager to show you all their presents from Santa Claus. I must reset my alarm clock.

Using the months of the year as a mnemonic you can either commit all 12 jobs to memory at one time or store them away one at a time as the need arises.

Heat Transfer
In the physical world heat transfer happens in one of 3 different ways:-

1. CONDUCTION,

2. CONVECTION,

3. RADIATION.

Stay with me, even if you are no science student. I will show you how I remember them. These are words that any reasonably well-informed person should know. Have an easy physics lesson and learn a bit more about remembering things at the same time.

1. Conduction
Hold the narrow end of a teaspoon which is immersed in a cup of your favourite hot drink and after a very short time the uncovered end that you are holding between your fingers warms up and becomes unbearably hot. The heat is transferred from one end of the spoon to the other by *conduction*.

It works this way. The heat causes the metal atoms making up the bowl of the spoon to vibrate. These vibrating atoms in turn cause the atoms next to them to vibrate, and this increased motion is passed (or conducted) rapidly along the stem to you, giving the sensation of heat moving along the spoon.

I remember that this effect is 'conduction' by picturing in my head a line of standing passengers on the lower deck of a crowded bus. The bus conductor lets another one on and calls; "Pass further down the bus, please," and everyone shuffles along. This is very unscientific – but seeing the atoms as people on a bus impelled to move by the CONDUCTOR tells me that the effect is 'conduction'.

2. Convection
Put a saucepan of water on the hot plate (ignoring the fact that the saucepan itself will get hot by conduction) and the heated water at the bottom of the pan will rise of its own

accord, making way for further cold water to move in and be heated in its turn. The circulating water is moving in *convection* currents. Warm air in a room acts similarly, moving away from the source of heat and warming up the whole room in a short while.

To remember 'convection' stretches my imagination. It is a specialised word, not one that crops up in everyday conversation. No mental picture comes readily to mind. The only other word I know with 'vec' in it is 'vector'. One meaning of vector is "a disease-carrying insect". So I think of a cloud of mosquitos or flies, very much like water or air convection currents. Thus my chain of thought goes:

currents of gas/water . . . like clouds of insects . . . vectors . . . convection currents.

3. Radiation

The transfer of heat from a hot to a colder body when they are not in contact (e.g. the Earth warmed by the Sun; or, on a much smaller scale, toast under a red-hot grill) is done by *radiation*.

This is easy to remember. Radiation occurs in space even though it contains no air. Heat radiation is, in fact, similar in character to radio or television waves or light waves. Waves are emitted by the hot body and transmitted through space, undetected until they fall on another body.

We know quite a lot these days about harmful radiations (like nuclear fallout) and of the safer kinds (e.g. sun-tanning in moderation). I simply recall that heat radiation is a sort of 'radiation'.

Jokes

The association of ideas is a good way to remember jokes. If you are one of those who say they have heard hundreds of jokes but can never think of one to tell, try filing jokes away in your mind in categories such as 'dog jokes', 'aeroplane jokes', jokes about 'spouses', and so on. Then, when the chatter drifts around to dogs, you can say; "Talking about dogs, there was this dog . . ."

Finally, on the subject of telling jokes, there is the story I first heard at school over 40 years ago. It concerns a newcomer in prison who hears the old lags taking it in turns over dinner to call out different numbers. After each one, there is a gale of laughter from the other inmates.

He turns to his neighbour and asks what is going on.

"We're telling funny stories," he replies. "Only, we know one another's jokes by heart after all this time together, so we've numbered them, and now we just call out the numbers."

The new boy thinks he will try, so he calls out a number. It is met with silence. He tries another. Still no sign of amusement.

"Why do they laugh at the others and not at me?" he demands.

"Ah," says his informant, "it must be the way you tell them."

LESSON 4
MNEMONICS

"I've a grand memory for forgetting, David . . ."
                    Robert Louis STEVENSON (1850–1894)

Mnemonics (pronounced "nee-monics") are devices such as rhymes, acronyms (code words), or other letter and word arrangements to assist remembering.

Acronyms

I was once paid to lecture to Trading Standards Officers on the subject of surveillance. The word S.U.R.V.E.I.L.-L.A.N.C.E. turned out, with some contrivance on my part, to have a letter for every topic I planned to talk to them about. I wrote these topics on cue cards to prompt me during my talk. This is what I did:-

```
S  –  hadowing suspects in the street
U  –  undercover observations in premises
R  –  eport writing
V  –  isits, official
E  –  vidence gathering
I  –  nformants
L  –  egislation
L  –  egal powers
A  –  ction to initiate prosecutions
N  –  ote taking
C  –  ourt appearances
E  –  ntrapment ("agent provocateur")
```

I also typed the 12 headings (as above) in the form of a handout for my students to keep as their reminder of the lesson.

Even rude words can serve as acronyms, as long as they remain in your mind and are not written down or otherwise broadcast so that they might offend others. There is one 4-letter word that spells out the ingredients of a criminal offence, and another that lists Nelson's famous sea victories in the order he achieved them. The more bizarre the mental assocation, the more indelible the imprint.

When I was a principal officer employed in the civic offices of a large London Borough, part of my job was compiling detailed and carefully reasoned written reports for consideration by chief officers and councillors. Most authorities have a set format, which everyone has off pat from continually using it, and I knew ours. Abruptly, the Access of Information Act, 1985, imposed upon Councils a requirement to include certain extra information in their reports, whereupon the layout of reports was changed – almost overnight – to make this possible. We all then had to learn the fresh format.

I wanted an acronym to fix it in my mind. Just 5 minutes doodling on a piece of scrap paper with pencil was enough. The new layout had to have paragraphs in the following sequence:-

HEADING

SUMMARY

DETAIL

FINANCIAL CONSIDERATIONS*

LEGAL CONSIDERATIONS

OTHER CONSIDERATIONS

RECOMMENDATIONS

DOCUMENT REFERENCES

CONTACT OFFICER
(with telephone extension)

* I changed this in my head to read 'Revenue' because I needed an 'R' in my acronym, which was:-

"H i S   D e a R   L O R D   C h r i s T"

Each capital letter reminds me of one of the headings. The phrase ensures they come in the right order. The words have no real meaning, except as a memory aid. It is an example of the odd way in which a problem in the office can be quickly solved. Incidentally, some chief officers I noticed were still muddling along uncertainly many months after the changed style of reporting came into use.

Acronyms are always better when their letters spell words, such as:-

> A.I.D.S.
> (acquired immune deficiency syndrome)
> L.A.S.E.R.
> (light amplifications by stimulated emission of
>   radiation)
> N.U.T.
> (National Union of Teachers)

Best of all are those spelling apt words, like:-

> A.S.H.
> (Action on Smoking & Health)
> S.E.A.
> (Shipbuilding Exports Association)
> P.A.C.T.
> (Private Agencies Collaboration Together (USA))

Be on the look-out for ready-made acronyms to use, or make up your own.

Poems
One of the most familiar rhyming mnemonics must be:-

> "Thirty days has September,
>   April,
>   June
>   & November.
> All the rest have thirty-one
> (excepting February alone,
> which has but twenty-eight days clear
> . . . and 29 in each Leap Year.)"

We may instinctively know if a month has 30 or 31 days in it; but I can still be unsure for a moment sometimes, until I run this rhyme through my head.

In the late Sir Alan P. Herbert's clever poem 'The Bowline' (already mentioned in Lesson 2), which I recite publicly from time to time, there is a chunk that I used to muddle up. As the poem is just 36 lines long, and 8 lines gave me trouble, it was something I had to sort out. Here is the bit I am talking about:-

> "What ancient hairy tar, how many centuries ago,
> Was author of the artifice we do not seem to know.
> Maybe old Captain Noah, scarce aware what he was at,
> Thus made a grass-rope ready when he sighted Ararat;
> Maybe 'twas wise Ulysses when he made the sailors fast
> Against the songs of Sirens with a bowline to the mast;
> Maybe by Captain Jason was the first example tied,
> That some industrious Argonaut might pain the *Argo*'s side;"

I used to mix up those references to Noah and Ulysses and Jason, quoting them out of sequence so that the tale did not run true. Then I spotted that the initial letters of their names were N.U.J. (National Union of Journalists). As long as I bear that in mind as I approach the troublesome part I am all right. Problem solved.

Stalagmites & Stalactites

They are those brittle fingers, like giant icicles, found in ancient caves. Created by limestone-rich water dripping in one spot, one kind projects upwards from the floor of the cave, while the other hangs down from the cavern ceiling. Which is which and how is each one spelt?

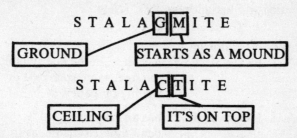

Elephants

Next time you go to a zoo have a look at the elephants. There are 2 kinds, Indian and African. At first glance they may seem identical but they do have many distinguishing features, for example the tips of their trunks, the bulge of their foreheads, and the way their spines curve. A keeper will tell you. The most obvious sign, for even the least observant chap like me is their ears.

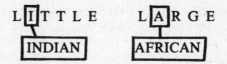

Spelling

You might be defeated spelling the odd word when you know no rule of grammar to help you. Often all you need is something to fix it in your mind. This Lesson is a mixture of various bits and pieces, a miscellany. Take that word "miscellany". We generally abbreviate it to 'Misc.' and everyone recognises what that means; but, if you want it spelt out in full for any reason, there is the immediate difficulty of how many 'l's and 'n's there are – also that 'c' stuck in the middle but silent. It helps to split it up as follows:-

M I S C – E L L A – N Y

This way you start off with 'Misc' (which you know). Then follows the woman's name 'Ella' (think of U.S. singer Ella Fitzgerald) and her address, 'NY' (New York).

Stationery & Stationary

S T A T I O N E R Y — has an 'e' in the last syllable but one, as in a scr(e)ed of writing on paper.

S T A T I O N A R Y — has an 'a' in the penultimate syllable, as in st(a)nding still.

Metre v. Meter

M E T R E — This is the basic unit of measuring length in the metric system and METRE contains the letters 'tr' just like me(tr)ic.

M E T E R — The measuring device is therefore spelt the other way.

Desert v. Dessert

D E S E R T — means – to abandon;
or, a waste region (hot or cold) with little or no vegetation or rain;
or, a deserved reward, punishment or recompense.
A desert is where you could be deserted (abandoned).
A desert has less of everything, except ice or sand, and so it is easy to

remember that it only has one 's'.

D E S S E R T   means – the course of fruit or sweet at the end of a dinner meal, eaten with a dessert spoon.
As the dessert spoons are kept with the rest of the cutlery in a kitchen dre(ss)er, it is appropriate that both words include the double 'ss'.

Latin

Every once in a while you can surprise even yourself by digging deep down into your memory to come up with some fact you were unaware you knew. My wife and I were watching an American film on T.V. and one of the actresses on screen said to another; "Welcome to the sorority."

"Welcome to the . . . what?" asked my wife.

"Sorority. It must mean sisterhood," I responded without any thought, although I had never heard the word before. Here is what happened. I did some Latin at school four decades ago and know all the words in column 1 below, along with their English equivalents in columns 2 & 3.

1. Latin	2. English	3. Adjective	4. Noun
PATER	FATHER	PATERNAL	PATERNITY
MATER	MOTHER	MATERNAL	MATERNITY
FRATER	BROTHER	FRATERNAL	FRATERNITY
SOROR	SISTER	SORORAL	? ? ? ? ?

I do not recall ever having been taught the word to complete column 4 (bottom right), but, watching the film, it surfaced instantly. So, it seems that memory not only provides a data base of raw facts. It can also generate processed intelligence.

Hyper or Hypo?

I once wrote an article on drowning, based upon my experiences as a Thames river policeman in the 1960s and as a Diploma holder of the Royal Life Saving Society, in which I referred to 'hypothermia' which is the abnormally low body temperature that can result from immersion in cold water or other very cold conditions. When it appeared in print, the spelling of this vital word had changed to 'hyperthermia'. Now 'hyper' and 'hypo', when prefixed to words, give them opposite meanings. So I was irritated. Then I realised that I was uncertain who was right, the printer or me. I had to look them both up in a dictionary – and I was correct all along. Fretting about it finally fixed the difference in my mind.

H Y P E R   means 'over' or 'above', as in the fairly familiar words –
hyperactive – excessively or abnormally active;
hyperbole – exaggerated or extravagant speech;
hypercritical – over critical, especially in trivial matters;
hyperextension – extension of a limb beyond the normal range of movement;
hypermarket – a very large supermarket with a greater range of goods;
hypersensitive – over sensitive;
hyperspace – more than 3 dimensions;
hypertension – high blood pressure.

Pick one of these expressions which you already know and use yourself, and you will see that the 'hyper' prefix must mean 'over' or 'above'. In the same way seize upon just one of the words below that you are familiar with and the meaning of the prefix 'hypo' will become obvious.

H Y P O   means 'under' or 'beneath', as in –
hypocauset – Roman underfloor
heating;
hypocrisy – insincerity, falseness (*less* than the truth);
hypochondria – neurotic conviction of
illness (to do with the upper abdomen
beneath the ribs);
hypodermic – beneath the skin;
hypoglycaemia – low blood sugar
hypothesis – a proposition stated as a
basis for argument or reasoning,
lacking evidence;
hypoxia – oxygen deficiency in the
tissues.

Clearly, the abnormally low body temperature that started this off must be 'hypothermia'.

Summer Time

In those E.E.C. countries where clocks are advanced in Summer, how boring it is to hear otherwise bright people twice a year unsure if the clocks go backwards or forwards the one hour necessary to put on official Summer Time and to take it off again. Fix it in your mind any way you like – but do something to get it straight. The following phrases do it for me:-

S P R I N G – *FORWARD* (the clocks go *ON* 1 hour)

F A L L* – *BACK* (take an hour *OFF*)

*(The picturesque American word for Autumn)

Note Taking

When we talk about memorising things, we usually mean

to keep stuff "in our heads" without taking any notes. Writing it down seems somehow cheating. Not at all. Use notes whenever convenient. Write shopping lists; compile cue cards for public speaking; keep a diary. If you work as a cashier/receptionist, make sure you have a list of fees & charges and/or opening hours handy. Housewives, leave notes for yourselves. Those self-adhesive memo pads, with leaves that can be stuck to almost any surface and then peeled off cleanly when no longer needed, are excellent.

"Don't forget to de-frost the fridge."
"Put the dustbin out."
"Cancel the papers."

You can even perk yourself up with exhortations when you are downhearted.
"Most of the things I worry about never actually happen."

Taking notes might not seem much like memory training but it can be. The time and effort spent deciding on a few key words for cue cards to lead you through the various stages of a speech or lecture, to avoid the embarrassment of drying-up midway, often ensure you sail through with little or no reference to those notes on the day. That way you appear to be a ready, off-the-cuff speaker, and your careful preparation is not obvious. Formulating your notes entailed using the 6 guiding principles and you therefore remembered much more of what you did.

A lot of my working life was spent on shiftwork with rostered leave days taken irregularly. I have also employed staff who worked like that. It was essential to keep a diary so as to plan ahead and be sure of being anywhere at the right time. Keeping careful notes of duty variations, it was surprising how often – when the time came around – I just knew what I was doing anyway. There was no need to look it up. Jotting it down had fixed it in my mind for instant recall. This, once again, is because it involved putting into practice the 6 guiding principles in such a way that I was memorising effortlessly.

Discarding Mnemonics

The bricklayer working at speed to earn performance-related pay and the gold medal winning Olympic sprint swimmer have something in common. The skills they acquired painstakingly, a bit-at-a-time, have been practised until they come automatically. Too much conscious thought would inhibit their performances. How they do what they do is grooved in by much repetition (practice makes permanent) and put "to the back of their minds"; that basic knowledge is then dealt with at a lower level of consciousness, leaving them free to consider strategy and tactics.

"We'll soon need a code word to remember all our code words," inexperienced students sometimes say to me. Not so. Learn from the bricklayer and the swimmer. Use an acronym or other mnemonic to memorise something you need. Later, after repeated use, you will find you no longer need the mnemonic. It has served its purpose and can be discarded. When you have looked at a few elephants and deduced their continents of origin from the size of their ears ('little' for India and 'large' for Africa – see page 43) the ears alone will signal India or Africa to you. 'Little' and 'large' will go unused. You will simply know. Cockney rhyming slang is like that. "Apples" are stairs (the rhyming bit ". . . and pears" is dropped); similarly, "lah-di" is cigar (from "lah-di-dah"). So code words come and go. Do not hang on to them unnecessarily.

The driving instructors at the Metropolitan Police training school in Hendon, London, teach a system of car control that keeps you always in the right place on the road, in the right gear, at the right speed, by means of the following sentence:-

CAN   MY   SAFETY   BE   GIVEN   AWAY?

The initial letters of the words stand for the 6 basic elements of driving technique, as I learnt it, namely:-

C – OURSE,

M – IRROR,

S – PEED,

B – RAKES,

G – EAR,

A – CCELERATION.

Each must be considered at the approach to every hazard, in the strict order laid down. At slow speeds in light traffic it is possible to recite the sentence and at the same time perform the various actions. For high performance driving, however, the words must be discarded and replaced by practised physical skill. Once the words have served their purpose, and neuro-muscular systems have learnt their routine, reflexes must be allowed to take over.

Memory training – you see – can also be harnessed to acquire physical, as well as mental, skills.

It sometimes seems that experts are superhuman. How can shorthand-typists convert what they hear and see so rapidly to the tips of their writing fingers and the code of squiggly outlines they draw? The answer is by pure stimulus-&-response, all intervening steps ruthlessly eliminated. The subject of the next lesson needs that sort of skill.

LESSON 5
MORSE CODE, etc.

"To kiss a miss is awfully simple.
To miss a kiss is simply awful.
Kisses spread disease, it's stated,
So kiss me dear – I'm vaccinated."

(Morse telegraphists' practice piece)

Modern Uses

You might like to learn the Morse code. If you are physically active, maybe adventurous, likely to be afloat in a boat, on foot up a mountain or rambling along a cliff-top, or similarly isolated beyond hailing distance of help, it could be a life-saver. Walkers, climbers, cavers, explorers, canoeists, yachtsmen and women, sea-anglers, scouts & guides, and all who put themselves in such situations, ought to be able to attract attention and signal their condition or predicament to others. Morse code can be flashed with a torch or even by rhythmically pulling a curtain to-&-fro across a lighted window. You can blow a whistle, toot a horn or wave a flag, depending upon whether you are in daylight or darkness.

"Help – leg broken."

"Boat holed. Sinking fast."

"O.K. No help needed."

You see how useful it can be. Of course, there has to be someone on the receiving end who can read your communication. All the more reason to give it a try. You could rescue someone else.

Back in the 1950s, when I learnt Morse as a young National Service soldier in the British Army's Royal Corps of Signals, large numbers of telegraphists were employed in commerce and industry and shipping (as well as the Armed Forces). We were almost as commonplace as shorthand typists. Fast and accurate international communications were accomplished that way.

Nowadays the beep-beep code of dots and dashes devised around 1838 by American painter and inventor Samuel Finley Breese Morse (1791–1872) is not used so much. UHF–FM radio transmissions and micro-chip technology have made it possible for the President of the United States of America to chat with astronauts in space and on the moon as if by telephone. The piercing staccato Morse notes are no longer necessary to overcome the signal distortions that often made voice communication incomprehensible in the old days. That is a pity because it is still a very useful skill to have in reserve.

Memorising the dots and dashes assigned to represent the letters of the alphabet, also the numerals 1 to 9 & 0, looks a mighty difficult undertaking. It is easier than it looks. See for yourself. First look at the numbers and you will quickly spot the logic behind them.

1.	· — — — —	6.	— · · · ·
2.	· · — — —	7.	— — · · ·
3.	· · · — —	8.	— — — · ·
4.	· · · · —	9.	— — — — ·
5.	· · · · ·	0.	— — — — —

Numbers

Each Morse symbol for a numeral has 5 units, the dots and dashes being closely related to the numbers they represent. Spend a few minutes with a pencil and paper trying them out and you will be convinced that you understand them and can remember them.

Letters

I was with 20 other trade training recruits, all aged 17–18, in a barrack room in Catterick Camp, Yorkshire, one Winter's evening when our corporal entered. He issued each one of us with a white card on which were printed the Morse alphabet symbols.

"Learn those blighters by tomorrow morning when you will be tested," he said. Then he left us to it.

Was he being cruel or kind, giving no tuition or hints as to how it could be done? I do not know. Anyway, we sat up late that night, working either in groups or alone according to preference. It was my first lesson, although I did not recognise it at the time, in making the 6 guiding principles work. What we soon discovered, my mates and I, was that some of the symbols are similar to others, or exact opposites, and that a few had an odd sound or rhythm that makes them easier to remember. We learnt them accordingly. You can do it too. See the grouped symbols that follow.

E	·	T	—
I	· ·	M	— —
S	· · ·	O	— — —
H	· · · ·		

(Note – S.O.S. was chosen as the international distress call because of the clear and unmistakeable difference between 3 dots for 'S' and 3 dashes for 'O'; not, as legend has it, because it stands for "Save Our Souls". Omit the double "s's" when sending it repeatedly. Just send . . . /— — —/ . . . /— — — / . . . , etc.)

A · —	B — · · ·
N — ·	V · · · —
D — · ·	F · · — ·
U · · —	L · — · ·
G — — ·	K — · —
W · — —	R · — ·

Some people connect the rhythm of 'F' with the sentence "Did it '*urt* you?" I picture the Morse for 'K' as the front view of an old-fashioned monoplane, with a round fuselage and the wings on each side. R.A.F. slang for a plane was "a kite" ('K' for kite).

Q — — · —	X — · · —
Y — · — —	P · — — ·

Morse 'Q' sounds a bit like the first 4 notes of our British national anthem God Save Our Gracious ('Q' for) Queen. I see 'X' as an aeroplane's propellor and the symbol as allied to 'K' (see 'K' for kite) but with a bigger fuselage. That leaves only 3 odd men out to be learnt.

C — · — ·
J · — — —
Z — — · ·

Morse telegraphists discussing the code do not say; "Dot, dash, dot." They speak it as it sounds when transmitted from a Morse buzzer, pronouncing a dash as 'daw" (as in the bird, jack*daw*) and clipping the final 't' off a dot (pronounced "dit") when it is followed by another note. It comes off the tongue more easily that way.

> 'L' is therefore "di-daw-di-dit."
> 'Z' is "daw-daw-di-dit."

Back in the barrack room, having done all we could to commit our card contents to memory, we slept on it. Early next morning we went over it again. When tested, to our relief, we got it more or less right. A few practice sessions and we acquired some fluency, although it was to take 6 months of daily practice of increasing speed and complexity, to reach the standard needed for operational work abroad in H.Q. and field units. You do not need that proficiency. You really should try the Morse code. You will exercise your brain and also gain a rare and valuable skill that could save a life, even your own.

It is easier to send Morse code than to receive it, because, when you know what is coming next, you have fractionally longer for the mental process of encoding letters into dots and dashes. Trying to turn them back into letters and words, when you are on the receiving end, is harder and it takes more practice. Most telegraphists can send faster than they can receive.

It is a convention widely observed by W/T operators that you should (a) never send faster than you can receive, and (b) never send faster than the person sending to you. Then it is seldom necessary to ask; "Please send more slowly."

The verse at the beginning of this chapter was deliberately composed as a hard test for even practised Morse operators. It uses a lot of 'e's, 'i's and 's's. These, as you know, are encoded as dots. Dots are transmitted much faster than dashes (you cannot rush 't's, 'm's and 'o's, or the numerals '8', '9' and '0'). So, go easy with words like "this", "whistle" and others like them. Give the receiver's mind time to register, decode and write them down.

The Morse Code

A	· —	N	— ·
B	— · · ·	O	— — —
C	— · — ·	P	· — — ·
D	— · ·	Q	— — · —
E	·	R	· — ·
F	· · — ·	S	· · ·
G	— — ·	T	—
H	· · · ·	U	· · —
I	· ·	V	· · · —
J	· — — —	W	· — —
K	— · —	X	— · · —
L	· — · ·	Y	— · — —
M	— —	Z	— — · ·
1	· — — — —	6	— · · · ·
2	· · — — —	7	— — · · ·
3	· · · — —	8	— — — · ·
4	· · · · —	9	— — — — ·
5	· · · · ·	0	— — — — —

Phonetic Alphabet

While you are at it, have a go at the international Phonetic Alphabet too. We all occasionally have to spell out a word to someone. Use the system adopted by the professionals and emergency services, police, fire brigades, ambulance crews, coastguards, airline pilots, seamen, soldiers, journalists, and so on. Why settle for anything less?

A – LPHA	N – OVEMBER
B – RAVO	O – SCAR
C – HARLIE	P – APA
D – ELTA	Q – UEBEC
E – CHO	R – OMEO
F – OXTROT	S – IERRA
G – OLF	T – ANGO
H – OTEL	U – NIFORM
I – NDIA	V – ICTOR
J – ULIET	W – HISKY
K – ILO	X – RAY
L – IMA	Y – ANKEE
M – IKE	Z – ULU

To spell the name Smythe over an indistinct telephone line, say: "S – Sierra, M – Mike, Y – Yankee, T – Tango, H – Hotel, E – Echo." Nobody can possibly mishear that.

There is no shortcut to learning the phonetic alphabet,

unless it is to use only 4 or 5 of the words until they become ingrained before going on to another batch. Hearing others speak them helps. You might also like to pick out groups of words that go together.

NAMES	PEOPLE	GEOGRAPHICAL LOCATIONS
CHARLIE	PAPA	INDIA
JULIET	YANKEE	LIMA
MIKE	ZULU	QUEBEC
OSCAR		
ROMEO		
VICTOR		

DANCES	CAR MODELS
FOXTROT	GOLF
TANGO	SIERRA

MISC.
BRAVO
ECHO
HOTEL
KILO
NOVEMBER
UNIFORM
WHISKY
X-RAY

GREEK LETTERS
ALPHA
DELTA

Code of Flag Signals

Still on the subject of signalling, if you are an amateur or professional sailor or waterman, a working knowledge of the international code of signal flags can be useful.

Learn the alphabet first. The 26 flag patterns and colours are as distinctly different as they can be, but that makes it easier to learn them. Pick out similar pairs, or opposites.

A & B, with dovetailed cut out silhouettes.
P & S, positive and negative images of one another.
R & X
K & H
C & W

A flag's colour, taken with its meaning as a signal, can be memorable. 'B' is red. It stands for "I am taking in, or discharging, or carrying dangerous goods". So, red stands for danger, perhaps explosives ('B' for BANG).

'A' is blue and white. It means "I have a diver down". I imagine blue water and white bubbles from the diver.

'Q'is yellow and means "My vessel is healthy and I request free pratique (quarantine)". Yellow could mean fever ('Q' for quarantine).

There are many more, apt associations that can be used to memorise the flags and link them with their meanings. Invent some for yourself.

(If you trace the outlines of the flags, and then colour them yourself, you will be well on the way to learning them. You need a nautical almanac to find out what signals can be made with them.)

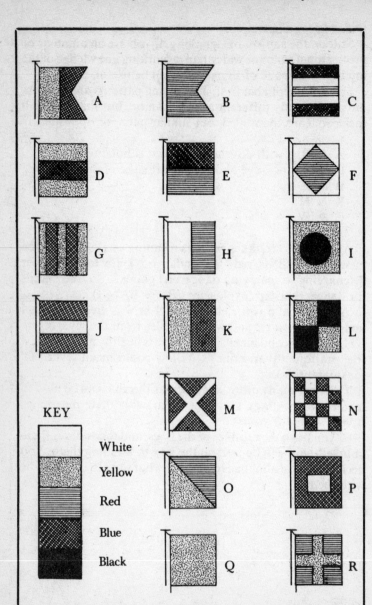

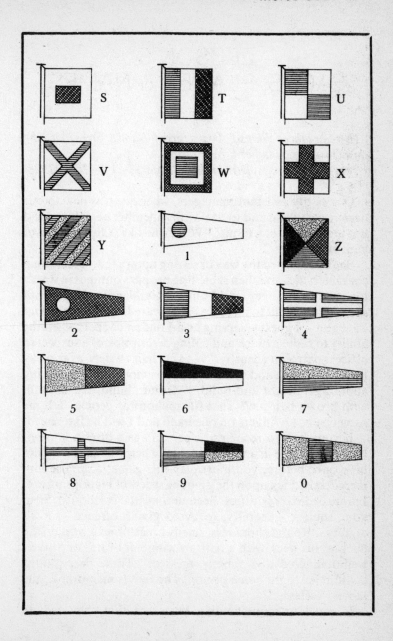

LESSON 6
FACES, PLACES & NAMES

"There are three things I always forget. Names, faces and – the third I can't remember."

Attributed to Italo SVEVO (1861–1928)

One of my assistant managers, when she was new to our organisation and had to deal with a member of staff she had not met, would say to me; "What's he like? Give me one of your summaries."

She had spotted my way of seizing upon a few outstanding characteristics and then sketching people's outlines in words by which a stranger could unfailingly identify them. Until she pointed it out to me, I was not aware I did it. I picked up the habit – I guess – serving as a London copper, when the ability to radio a quick and telling description of a suspect to officers patrolling nearby (". . . very hairy wrists, a far-away look in his eyes, and sniffs a lot") was more use than talking about age, height and build. "Medium build, 172 cm tall, with brown hair . . ." That fits millions of people. Tell me someone has 6 fingers on one hand and I will be interested.

If you want to recognise a person again after a lapse of time and maybe in another locality, when you have met him only once before, you must play this game. Appraise him mercilessly. Pick upon the unique aspects of his appearance. Ignore ordinary features. Become a mental cartoonist. Strip your subject – secretly, to avoid giving offence – of all dignity. "Round shoulders, smelly breath, and a wart on the back of his neck with a hair growing out of it:" or "quiet, well-mannered and soberly dressed." These descriptions could refer to the same person. The first is memorable, the second useless.

If someone's outstanding traits are that they radiate

charm and kindliness, look angelic and always smell alluring, then say so. Most of us, alas, have quite a few flaws for the sharp observer to pick on. Me? well, I'm 50-ish, often look far older, bald, with small ears. I talk a lot, waving my hands about as I do so. My nose is like a lump of putty and I peer over a pair of half-lens spectacles.

We need to recognise faces again (1) within a short time, later at the same party, business seminar, or other outing; and (2) after a substantial lapse of time, often in a totally different place. Two approaches are possible.

1. The same day, you might safely take notice of an elaborate hair-do, facial tan or make-up, signs of illness, ungainly weight distribution or skinniness. These will not change within a few hours.

2. Over any length of time, however, such signs could disappear. A beard might be shaved off overnight. A liking for clothes of a certain style or colour can change. To remember someone long-term we must select features of that person which are unlikely to change greatly. The shape of a nose, eyes, ears, mouth, chin, cheeks, or hands, will stay more or less the same from one year to the next. Adult height will not alter (except for a slight decrease with ageing). Date and place of birth never change, although a liar might tell you something different. Apparent age is often a better guide than real age. A 65-year-old with crowned teeth, suntan and jogging suit, can appear 50. A schoolgirl, dressed the part, may look 20-plus.

    My advice is to go for baldness, natural colouring and skin texture, warts, lumps and bumps, deformities, imperfections. Latch on to nervous tics and fidgety movements, noisy breathing, obsessive behaviour, speech oddities, posture, demeanour, and funny walks.

Faces & Places

You will generally want to link face and form with where

you came across them. We have all, I am sure, been hailed in the street by; "Hello, fancy seeing you here." Then follows a tricky few minutes of chat pretending you know who it is when you have not a clue who on earth it might be. How can you link an appearance with the place where you committed it to memory? No great imagination is needed.

I was visited recently by a salesman. He was smartly turned-out in blazer and slacks, with a clean shirt and formal tie. Ignore that. If I bump into him away from work he might be informally dressed. He had tightly curled hair, fairly unusual on a man, but it was not natural and so it too could change with time. Nothing worth concentrating on so far. Then he reached out his right hand to shake mine and I saw his thumb was missing. He acted unselfconsciously about it and told me – because I asked (starting to bring the 6 guiding principles into play) – that he had lost it in an industrial accident. Later in our conversation he mentioned his hobby was photographing wildlife outdoors at night. That could raise problems, I thought to myself, for a man whose manual dexterity was limited. This fixed firmly in my mind that he was a photographer. Our business together concerned an estimate for replacing swimming pool hall lighting in my leisure centre. I asked what sort of lighting he used for his night photography. After only a few minutes in his company I was confident I had absorbed enough to know him again on sight, when I would promptly think of his photography, and – by association – my pool hall lighting. His first name was Michael (Mike for short) and it is an easy link for me between lighting and another electrical installation of mine, the public address system, with microphones (mikes). In this way I would know for certain that he was the salesman called Mike who came to see me at work about lighting.

He would remember me. He is a good salesman, who probably keeps a card index with me in it. As soon as he returned to his car from our meeting he would have noted what we talked about, to refresh his memory before we met next time. We customers like to feel special and to be treated like old friends, even when we know it is contrived. People warm to you when you show an interest in them.

Names

We English are in my experience pathetic when it comes to remembering the names of people we have just met. Most of us are better with faces. Perhaps other nations are as bad. This weakness is often blamed upon our traditional reserve that makes us reluctant to ask for a name to be repeated when first we hear it, or to admit later that we failed to grasp it. Well, shyness and pride aside, it is sheer mental laziness and lack of systematic application.

I employed at one of my swimming pools an Iraqi lifeguard whose name was Natheer GEORGE. George was his surname. His first name was Natheer. Everyone but me called him "George" because it sounded like a Christian name and, anyway, they had never really found out how you said Natheer. They knew it was wrong but went on doing it, without even asking whether or not he liked it. Strangers overhearing them assumed George was his first name. ("First name" is, incidentally, a more tactful term than christian name in our increasingly agnostic and multi-racial society.) People in other departments would ring me to ask; "Do you have a George someone-or-other in your section?" He good-naturedly answered to his new label but must have been irked occasionally that we could not be bothered to cope with his real first name. I used it, but that caused difficulties because others did not know who I was talking about. What nonsense.

The effort of learning a person's name is amply repaid. Folk like you to use their names. They make no allowance for a poor memory for names but assume it is rudeness or a lack of interest in them. Maybe it is.

It is better to use a name and make a mistake. At least you can be corrected and so learn what it really is. Then get it right. My late father used to call me "Foster", which is my elder brother's name. As we are a generation apart in age, he grew up and left home before I was really on the scene. Dad had had a decade-and-a-half when the juvenile male in the house was called Foster and he just never shook off the habit.

Use the 6 guiding principles. Take time over a new name. Get clear in your mind what is being said to you. Have it spelled out. Talk about it. Use it from the outset. Tell it to others.

Mind you, I sometimes make a hash of things. I confess it. Two female cleaners worked for me. Pam and Jan. Pam worked mornings and Jan evenings. Because I was an office worker coming in at 8 a.m. and leaving by 5 p.m. most days, I saw Pam to chat to every day. I rarely saw Jan, except when she came early or I worked late. Time and again, when this happened, I addressed her as "Pam". Sometimes I knew it was wrong as I uttered it. More often she had to remind me. How embarrassing. It was as bad as my father calling me by my brother's name. Mindless reflex, hard to overcome. I resolved finally that every time I saw Jan, and before opening my mouth, I would think to myself "Just a nano-second" (a nano-second = one thousand millionth of a second, or 10^{-9} second). This phrase would not only make me pause, but the initial letters of the 3 words spelt the name J.A.N. Silly ideas like that can prove most effective.

There are a few rare professional memory experts who give truly amazing demonstrations of their technical powers, recalling the faces and names of perhaps a hundred or more guests at a dinner or meeting, having been introduced to each one in turn only briefly, earlier in the proceedings. Others, performing on stage, can tell you of past events in great detail by answering questions called out by the audience. Some magicians appear to know entire books off by heart. Many are genuine. Some are clever showmen and women, who still deserve our applause and admiration for their showmanship. Not one of them is as miraculous as we let ourselves believe. Human brain potential is far beyond the timid limits most of us accept as satisfactory. One psychologist stated on a recent radio chat show that he and many of his colleagues now believed we operate on as little as

2% of our real capabilities. That is incredible.

Without aspiring to master the names of crowds, you can do a lot better with the few individuals you do meet for the first time each week. "I can remember faces but I'm no good at names," is a common cry. That is no excuse. Apply yourself. Use the 6 guiding principles.

1. MINUTES, not seconds	Take your time. Do not rush introductions. Slow them down.
2. EVALUATE	Think, is it a common or rare name? Does it fall into a particular category (see lists 1 to 6, following)?
3. MAKE AN EFFORT	Write it down (seeing & hearing). Check you have it right by questions.
4. ORDER THE DATA	Have it spelled out. Ask for a business card. Is it on headed letter paper, in the telephone directory, or a trade journal?
5. REINFORCE	Take every opportunity to use the name. Introduce the person to others.
6. CURIOSITY	Ask the person about himself. Subject him to a mild and kindly interrogation.

Note – Eyes are better than ears because they feed our brains with images rather than sounds. We can turn words into pictures by writing names down, taking a business card, etc.

Nobody ever misspells my first name Geoffrey. There are, of course, 2 ways of spelling it. But people unfailingly ask me how I spell it.

> "Is that with a 'G' or a 'J'?"
> "G."
> "G-e-o?"
> "That's right."
> "Are there 2 'ff's?"
> "Yes."
> ". . . and that's 'r-e-y', isn't it?"
> "Correct."

Then they never get it wrong. Once they have established that I am 'Geoffrey' and not 'Jeffrey' it is straightforward forever more.

But the Budworth family suffers unending irritation from having its surname misspelt and misspoken, even by those who have at some time or other seen it written down. I type it on my letters, yet back come replies addressed "Dear Mr . . . Butterworth,

> Budsworth,
> Buckworth,
> Bloodworth,
> Bidworth,
> Budsworthy,
> etc., etc., etc.

The writers just do not pay attention, or else they think they know best. It does annoy me. We really should give consideration to getting names right. And it can be done. A few years ago I took on the stage name 'Bud WORTH'. People have no difficulty with it at all, whether they see it written down or merely hear it spoken. It is the same name, spelt the same way, only broken into 2 parts. That is what makes the difference. It is easier to grasp. Try it yourself with names you find hard.

You watch a film. As part of the action there is a knock on the door. An actress opens it.

"Mrs. Smith?" enquires the caller. "Mrs. *Jennifer* Smith?"

Immediately we hear this emphasis upon correctly establishing both first- and sur-names we know the caller is an official in plain clothes, probably a policeman or maybe a town hall bureaucrat. Playwrights and directors use the device every time. We may have considered it a dreary approach; but, as we now wrestle with trying to pin down names in our minds, it is a good example to follow. Professionals in the name game, policemen, social workers, reporters, local government officers, are experts. We can learn from them.

As a young probationer constable I was taught the following routine.

"What is your full name, please?"

"Anne-Marie Betty."

"Is Betty your surname?"

"Yes." (We had to underline or print surnames so that there was no confusion later when, as in this instance, a surname might also be used as a first name.)

". . . and is Anne-Marie your only first name?"

"No. My middle name is Peggy, but I hardly ever use it."

"Is it actually Peggy, or is that a variation of Margaret?"

"No. Peggy."

"So it's Anne-Marie Peggy BETTY."

"Yes."

"How do you spell Anne-Marie?"

"A-n-n-e, hyphen, M-a-r-i-e."

". . . and Peggy? Is that P-e-g-g-y?"

"Yes."

"And Betty . . . B-e-t-t-y?"

"That's right."
"Thank you, Mrs. Betty. Now, what is your full postal
    address, please?"

And so on. It seems a long rigmarole for something so
simple. But that is the very point. Unless you concentrate
and make a big thing of it – taking minutes, not seconds, and
using all the guiding principles – it is all too easy to make
mistakes with names. Labour the business as I have
suggested and you only have to do it once.

LIST 1

Some surnames can be associated with characters, in fact
or fiction, who are renowned for one reason or another.
True, we are unlikely to be introduced to an Einstein,
Michelangelo, Tolstoy, Vasco da Gama or Oedipus, but we
might meet one of the following:-

A D A M	The world's first man.
B O W D L E R	Thomas (1754–1825), a British editor who came to represent prudish expurgation of classic literary works.
C H U R C H I L L	Winston Leonard Spencer (1874–1965), British statesman, writer, and inspiring war leader.
D A V I S	Dwight F. (1879–1945), who in 1900 donated a cup for the nation winning an annual international lawn tennis championship.
E P S T E I N	Sir Jacob (1880–1959), British sculptor.
F O R S Y T H	William (1737–1804), British

botanist associated with importing the Chinese flowering forsythia shrub to Britain.

GARLAND

Judy (1922–1969), American film and stage star and singer, best known as Dorothy in the 1939 film *Wizard of Oz*.

HENRY

Joseph (1797–1878), American physicist whose name was given to the S.I. unit of electrical inductance.

ISHERWOOD

Christopher (1904–1986), English novelist whose portrayal of the 1930s Berlin led to the musical *Cabaret*.

JOHNSON

Dr. Samuel (1709–1784), British writer and lexicographer.

LOGAN

James Harvey (1841–1928), U.S. judge who developed the hybrid raspberry called the loganberry.

MURPHY

"Murphy's Law". If something can go wrong, it will; and in the worst possible way.

NEWTON

Sir Isaac (1642–1727), the great English mathematician and physicist known for his treatise on gravitation.

ORWELL

George (1903–1950), real name Edward Arthur BLAIR, best known for his novel *1984* and also the political allegory *Animal Farm*.

PRESLEY   Elvis Aaron, (1935–1977) the
               'King' of rock-&-roll music.

QUISLING   Vidkun (1887–1945), Norwegian
               traitor, executed for having
               served as minister president
               under Nazi occupation in World
               War II.

RALEIGH   Sir Walter (c1554–1618),
               Elizabethan explorer, sailor,
               writer, poet and historian, held in
               the Tower of London until finally
               executed.

SAMSON   Biblical strong man.

TESLA   Nikola (1856–1943), Croatian
               born U.S. electrical engineer
               whose name has become the S.I.
               unit of magnetic flux density.

ULBRICHT   Walter (1893–1973), East
               German statesman who erected
               the Berlin Wall.

VANBRUGH   Sir John (1664–1726), English
               architect and playwright.

WRIGHT   Orville (1871–1948) and Wilbur
               (1867–1912), U.S. pioneer
               aviators.

If you imagine the person you have just met dressed as the more famous owner of the surname, acting as he or she acted, doing the things he or she did, the likelihood that you will remember the person is greatly strengthened.

LIST 2

Other surnames are notable because they are instantly

associated with an invention, some patent manufactured product, an historical event, or some-such. If you meet a Mr. Everest, imagine him attired in climbing gear up a large mountain and the name will stick. Mr. Newton can be pictured inundated with apples raining down upon him. Thompsons can be remembered as gangsters carrying 'Tommy guns' in violin cases and acting out St. Valentine's Day massacres.

ATLAS
A Titan giant in Greek mythology, condemned to support the heavens upon his shoulders, whose name is now given to any volume of maps or other specialised plates (e.g. anatomy).

BOYCOTT
Captain Charles C. (1832–1897), an unpopular land agent in County Mayo, Ireland, who was ostracised by his tenants, giving rise to the verb 'boycott' for protesting by refusing to deal with someone.

CARDIGAN
A uni-sex knitted jacket, buttoned or with a V-neck, named after the 7th Earl of Cardigan, James Thomas Brudenell (1797–1868). British cavalry officer.

DIESEL
Rudolf (1858–1913), the German engineer who pioneered the 4-stroke engine diesel cycle.

EVEREST
Sir George (1790–1866), English surveyor-general of India, after whom the world's highest mountain is named.

FUCHS   Leonhard (1501–1566), German
                botanist whose name is given to
                the genus of Fuchsia shrubs.

GARIBALDI   Giuseppe (1807–1882), Italian
                soldier and nationalist leader
                after whom both a style of
                woman's blouse and a currant
                biscuit have been named.

HOOVER   Herbert Clark (1874–1964) after
                whom Colorado's 'Boulder Dam'
                was renamed: also a generic
                name for vacuum cleaners, from
                the U.S. manufacturer William
                Henry Hoover (1849–1932).

JACUZZI   Candido (c1903–1986), Italian
                born, who is now firmly
                associated with remedial spa
                baths relying upon water swirling
                around to provide gentle massage
                for the bathers.

KELVIN   William Thomson, 1st Baron
                (1824–1907), British physicist and
                inventor, after whom the S.I. unit
                of thermodynamic temperature is
                named.

LYNCH   William (1742–1820), U.S.
                Virginian vigilante, and Charles
                (1736–1796), planter and J.P.,
                both of whom are alleged to have
                hanged suspects without due
                process of law.

MACKINTOSH   Charles (1760–1843), Scottish
                chemist, after whom the 'mac'
                or 'mack' raincoat is named.

NEGUS

Arthur (late), English antique dealer known from his many T.V. appearances: also the title of the Ethiopian emperors; and a special drink of port or sherry supposed to be named after Colonel Francis Negus (d1732).

OCKHAM

William of . . . (died c1349), English philosopher and Franciscan monk who urged a principle of philosophical and scientific discussion now oddly known as 'Ockham's razor'.

PLIMSOLL

Samuel (1824–1898), the M.P. whose support of the 1876 Merchant Shipping Act led to the set of hull markings on sea-going merchant ships indicating legal loading, thus saving seamen's lives by reducing needless losses due to overloading.

QUEENSBERRY

John Sholto Douglas, 8th Marquis of . . . (1844–1900), who developed the modern boxing code of rules now generally synonymous with fair play in any activity.

RAGLAN

Fitzroy James Henry Somerset, 1st Baron Raglan (1788–1855), British Field Marshal credited with the coat whose sleeves go right to the collar without shoulder seams.

SHRAPNEL

Henry (1761–1842), English

artillery officer who invented the anti-personnel projectile that exploded in the air, to send shell fragments or other missiles collectively to do increased hurt.

THOMPSON   John (1860–1940), U.S. army officer and co-inventor of the .45 calibre Thompson sub-machine (or 'Tommy') gun.

Van der
WAALS   Johannes D. (1837–1923), Dutch physicist, whose name is given to the weak inter-atomic or inter-molecular attraction arising from the interaction of dipoles induced in neighbouring atoms or molecules.

WELLINGTON   Arthur Wellesley, 1st Duke (The Iron Duke) (1769–1852), British soldier–statesman and prime minister, who gave his name to the calf or knee-length "gumboot".

ZIMMERMAN   Whimsically, a person using the lightweight, sturdy, metal frame designed to support and aid the elderly or disabled when walking.

To associate names like this, you need wide general knowledge and experience. Mine will be different from yours. Use your own whenever possible.

LIST 3

It is easier when people have surnames that are the names

of actual feelings, times, places, objects or positions (i.e. of status) and so on. Visualise Dukes as dukes; Haddocks as haddocks; Parrots as exotic jungle birds. See Quilters making bedspreads; Ushers robed in courts of justice or churches. Give your imagination full rein. Your memory for names must improve.

ARCHER	ABBOT	ALMOND
ASH	AGATE	AXE
BARBER	BAKER	BERRY
BARROW	BELL	BISHOP
CHAMPION	COOK	CHRISTMAS
CLIFF	CHILD	CLOVER
DEVONSHIRE	DIAMOND	DENT
DUFF	DUKE	DOWN
ENGLAND	EARL	EDGE
ESSEX	EDEN	EAVES
FAIR	FARE	FALCONER
FIELD	FELL	FARMER
GATE	GARDINER	GARLAND
GEARING	GLASS	GORE
HANDS	HADDOCK	HALL
HEDGE	HAM	HAIL
INCH	IRONMONGER	INGLE
IRELAND	INSTANCE	INKPEN
JAY	JACK	JEANS
JEWEL	JOY	JUDGE

KEY	KEEL	KEEP
KITCHEN	KING	KETTLE
LORD	LAMB	LANE
LARK	LEMON	LUCK
MALLET	MARSHAL	MASON
MEAD	MAYOR	MOUNTAIN
NIGHTINGALE	NURSE	NIPPER
NODES	NOON	NUN
ONION	OAK	OLIVE
ORCHARD	ORGAN	OSPREY
PARROT	PAGE	PAIN
PARSON	PARISH	PATCH
QUAY	QUAIL	QUARRY
QUICK	QUILTER	QUIRK
RECORD	RAINBOW	RANGER
READER	REED	RICE
SALMON	SANDS	SAVAGE
SCORE	SEAL	SHILLING
THORN	TACK	TANKARD
TONGUE	TEMPLE	THATCHER
USHER		
VENUS	VALE	VALENTINE
VINE	VEAL	VANE
WALKER	WATERS	WARREN
WOOD	WEIR	WINTER
YEOMAN	YARD	YORK
YOUNGHUSBAND	YOUNGMAN	YULE

LIST 4

Some surnames stretch the imagination and must be broken up before you can see a picture. Still, Armstrongs may be visualised as weightlifters, body-builders, arm-wrestlers or blacksmiths; Goldrings can be mentally bedecked with rings through their noses and ears, on every finger, and around their necks, wrists and ankles, until they can barely walk with the weight; Peckhams peck ham; Lightfoots have strobe 'disco' flashing lights on each and every toe of their feet; Waghorns wag devilish or beastly horns.

ARM/STRONG	BUS/BRIDGE	CORD/WELL
DEAR/DEN	ELPHIN/STONE	FRANK/HAM
GOLD/RING	HONEY/BONE	INGLE/FIELD
JAY/COCK	KILL/MAN	LIGHT/FOOT
MAR/CHANT	NEW/PORT	OAK/HILL
PECK/HAM	QUARTER/MAN	RING/WOOD
SHRUBS/HALL	TOWNS/END	UNDER/WOOD
VOW/LES	WAG/HORN	YOUNG/MAN

LIST 5

Abstract names take a real effort to memorise. Mr. & Mrs. Kentish can be pictured in some Kent location you know well (or even one you imagine, although you have never been there). Welches can be thought of as Welsh (by adopting the alternative spelling), or absconding bookmakers ('welsh' means to swindle someone by defaulting and avoiding payment of a debt or wager).

ABLE	BLACK	CLEAR
DEAR	EARLY	FRENCH
GREY	HIGH	IDLE
JOLLY	KENTISH	LONG
MALE	NOBLE	OGLES
PETTY	QUICKLY	READ
SHARP	TICKLE	WELCH
YOUNG		

LIST 6

Finally there are surnames that do not readily yield any sense at all. Now, however, having had some practice at conjuring up striking images, it should be possible for you to summon up images out of these too. For example, the name 'Keyhoe' could be represented by a scene where a farmer used a KEY to HOE a field of weeds. 'Sharma' could be remembered by a snake charmer, abbreviated to S'harmer (then spelt Sharma). 'Tooke' can be imagined stealing (taking) a giant letter 'E' from a sign.

AINSWORTH	ALBERY	ALLISON
APLIN	ASPINALL	AVERY
BARDEN	BASSETT	BOAKES
BOHANE	BOYCE	BRAITHWAITE
CAWKHILL	CHISHOLM	CHOWN
COWAN	CRAIG	CRUTTENDEN
DEMEZA	DIGGINS	DITZELL
DIVALL	DOWDALL	DUDDLE
EADE	EDMEADE	ELDRIDGE
ELLISON	EVERETT	EVERINGTON
FAHY	FAIRCLOUGH	FITZSIMMONS
FOTHERGILL	FRASER	FRIEDLANDER
GARBUTT	GASSON	GHINN
GLOCK	GOMEZ	GOSBEE
HARTLEY	HAWES	HENNELL
HEPPELL	HOMDEN	HULME
IBBETSON	INGRAM	INGLIS
ISAACS	ISTED	IVENS
JACQUES	JAGELMAN	JESSOP

JOHAL JOBLING JUPP

KEHOE KEMSLEY KILLICK
KITTLE KNAGGS KRAFFT

LAMBOURNE LEAHY LEDERMAN
LEIPNIK LENG LEYLAND

McGONAGLE MANKTELOW MANSER
MEIKLE MEREDITH MORTIMER

NEWELL NOCK NOLAN
NORWOOD NOVAK NOYES

OBBARD OLLERENSHAW ORMSTON
ORSBOURN ORTON OUTTRIM

PADGETT PEARSALL PHILLIPS
PICKERING PLAYLE POOLEY

QUAIFE QUANTRILL QUARRINGTON
QUELCH QUINNELL QUITTENDEN

RANCE REYNOLDS RICHARDS
RIMINGTON ROFFE ROSSITER

SANTER SEAGER SELBY
SHARMA SHERWIN SPARLING

TAPSELL TEDHAM TICKNER
TINDELL TOOKE TOPLISS

UDEN UMFREVILLE UNWIN
UREN USMAR UZZELL

VARNEY VILLIERS VINCENT
VOGT VOLLER VOUSDEN

WARRILOW WATTENBACK WEDDELL
WHIDDETT WOLSTENHOLME WRATTEN

YAPP YEARSLEY YEO
YORKE YOUELL YUSUF

ZUTSHI

LESSON 7
THE 't-for-1' CODE

"Tell me not in mournful numbers . . ."
           H. W. LONGFELLOW (1807–1882)

Before going on with this lesson, I have just noticed Longfellow's initials. As he wrote the poem 'HiaWatha' I shall always remember them by that fact from now on. It is an opportune example of the way association can occur quickly and easily.

Learning words is easy when one idea leads logically to the next. It is even easier when the words rhyme, especially so if they are set to music. That is why pop songs get inside our heads through sheer repetition and little or no effort by us.

Prose that makes little or no sense such as legal or technical texts and officialese, on the other hand, must first be simplified. Numbers can be even more of a problem to remember, if you do not regularly work with them or have an interest in figures. Fortunately there is a way to make memorising them fast and reliable, the most powerful trick I know for developing a remarkable memory.

It is a system which substitutes letters of the alphabet for numerals so that you can READ NUMBERS AS WORDS. This way you can quickly learn lists of numbers or objects, the order of playing cards, even impress upon your mind difficult chunks of written text. It is known as the "t-for-1" code, because the figure '1' becomes encoded as the letter 't' (or the phonetically similar 'd'). It is believed the code goes back to at least the 1600s. Since then it has been used by all kinds of people and is taught in colleges and business institutes.

I came across it by chance when I was 25, learnt the code in half an hour on a train journey from London Bridge to Greenwich, and in a few days was fluent enough to use it. It has served me well for over 25 years. It is not complicated and you can grasp it as easily as I did. This is it:-

1	2	3	4	5	6	7	8	9	0
t	n	m	r	l	j	k	f	p	s
d					g	g	v	b	z
					dg	c			c
					ch	ck			
					sh	que			

Note – The 'g' used instead of '6' is a soft one (as in George), whereas the 'g' and 'c' used for '7' are hard consonants (such as in Greenland and Camelot).

You can learn the 't-for-1' code in a few minutes once you spot a connection between each figure and the letter replacing it.

t is 1 . . . . because both are written with a single downstroke.

n is 2 . . . . because both are written with a single curve.

m is 3 . . . . because both have 2 distinct curves.

r is 4 . . . . if you can roll your 'r's in speech, then 'r' can become the dominant letter "fou*rrrrr*".

l is 5 . . . . Latin 'L' is 50.

j is 6 . . . . 'j' can be handwritten as a mirror-image of 6.

k is 7 . . . The first upright stroke of a capital 'K' can be written like a 7.

f is 8 . . . . . . A longhand 'f' has 2 closed loops like an 8.

p is 9 . . . . 'p' can be written as the reverse of a 9.

s is 0 . . . The letter that is all curves represents the figure that is all curves.

Encoding Numbers

To read a number as a word, replace each of the figures by one of the consonants shown beneath them; then insert any vowels which will make a word. Take as an example '12'. Twelve becomes t-something-n (or d-something-n), so a lot of words are possible.

TAN	TEN	TIN
TON	TUN	DAN
DEN	DIN	DON
DUN		

Vowels do not count, so you can also add them at the beginning or end to make further words.

TINA	TINE	ETON
TONE	TUNA	TUNE
ADEN	EDEN	ODIN
DANE	DENE	DINE
DONE	DUNE	ATTUNE*

* The "tt" is still only '1' as the code works by sound and NOT by how the word is spelt.

The only strict rules are that you must keep the 't' (or 'd') and 'n' sounds in the right order (to avoid confusing 12 with 21 etc.), and you must never accidentally introduce any letter that represents another numeral. Now any one of those words decodes and can be read as 12, and only as 12. Which word I choose, therefore, to represent 12 depends upon why I need to remember that number.

If I want to recall that my nephew Daniel is now 12 years old, that is straightforward. I file away in my mind; "Dan is 12". Too easy.

Suppose you are contriving to date someone of the opposite sex. You overhear the address and want to be sure of remembering the house number in the street without giveaway note-taking. You could use TAN if he was brown, or DANE if she was blonde, or EDEN if you pictured the two of you living happily ever after. It is about mental pictures. You must pick a word that springs to mind the moment you think of him or her . . . and it must decode to 12.

I have not so far mentioned consonants 'h', 'w', 'x', or 'y'. Like vowels, these can be used without affecting the numerical value of words, making more possibilities from 12.

TANNOY	TINNY
WOTAN	WOODEN
HIDDEN	HEARTEN

A general knowledge question featured in one brand-name quiz game, asks how many steps lead to 221b Baker Street, home of the fictional detective Sherlock Holmes. The answer is 17. How memorable. The slang abbreviation 'tec' (for detective) decodes to 17.

More than one theatrical mind-reading act has depended upon this code. I can read your mind at this moment. You are thinking this is very involved just to memorise a few numbers. But do read on. The code can also help you to learn prose.

Prose

To qualify in the management of baths and leisure centres my professional institute's examiners required me to know something of the Sports Council. An absolute essential was to be able to reproduce in an answer paper the Council's 4 published 'Aims'. The only way to do that was word perfect. The Aims of the Sports Council are to:-

1.   *Promote general understanding* of the social importance and value of sport and physical recreation;

2.   *Increase provision* of new sports facilities and stimulate fuller use of existing facilities;

3.   *Encourage wider participation* in sport and physical recreation as a means of enjoying leisure;

4.   *Raise standards* of performance.

The Sports Council does not actually number its Aims 1, 2, 3 & 4. I did so to help me apply the code. I only memorised the bits italicised above, and these headings acted as cues for me to recall the rest.

Here is what I did. No. 1 encodes (among other things) as 'tea'. I picture in my mind's eye a great big cup of steaming brown tea. To cope with the words 'Promote general understanding' I concentrate hard, for a few seconds only, on a mental image of an Army GENERAL. He is a ridiculous little figure, barely one foot tall, STANDING UNDERNEATH his horse. He is drinking that cup of tea. Some V.I.P.s are PROMOTING him to Field Marshal (or whatever they promote generals to). Now, if you ever fire at me; "Quick, give me the first Aim of the Sports Council," I come right back with; "No. 1 – Promote general understanding of . . ." Do you understand? Just as with all association of ideas, so with the 't-for-1' code, you must link together 2 vivid mental pictures. Only now, one is a number and the other the fact you wish to recall. Told one, you recall the other. If you had asked me where 'Promote general understanding' comes in the list order, I cannot fail to say; "No. 1." The 2 pictures (tea and the general) are inseparable.

Here is how I memorised the other 3 aims.

No. 2 can be represented by the word 'Noah'. He took 2 of every species aboard the Ark to propagate them. I form a childish image of Noah and his Ark surrounded by multiplying creatures ('Increasing provision . . .').

I use 'May' (the month) for No. 3, picturing May blossom trees in a garden walk I knew well in my childhood town of Bournemouth. Mental associations must be like that. Your own are best. 'Encourage wider participation . . .' is a vague phrase to memorise. It took some imagination to link it with May blossom. Then it came to me. That particular walk is a tourist attraction. Each year, when the blossom is at its best, the local papers tell everyone to go and see them while the display lasts. This encourages the maximum number of people to go and enjoy the sight ('Encouraging wider participation . . .').

No. 4 I read as 'Ray'. I imagine the sun's rays falling on a banner being hauled up a flag mast ('Raising standards . . .').

You can astonish people with your memory if you adopt this code. A good memory – I repeat – is NOT a gift; it is a reward. It works when you concentrate, forming pictures in your mind. The 't-for-1' code works best when you turn numbers into words that are *nouns*. Nouns are easier to picture.

Keywords

When you become quick at making memorable – even outrageous – mental links, it can then be simpler to use the same word for the same number all the time. Rather than wasting time casting around in the hope of finding a peculiarly apt word, settle for the same one and make it fit what you want to commit to memory. For the numbers 1 to 100 I use the following 100 key words.

1	Tea	6	Shaw
2	Noah	7	Key
3	May	8	Fee
4	Ray	9	Bay
*5	"Lee-O"	10	Toes

11	Tot	49	Rope
12	Tan	50	Lace
13	Team	51	Light
14	Taro	52	Lane
15	Tool	53	Lamb
16	Tich	54	Lair
17	'tec	55	Lily
18	Toffee	56	Latch
19	Tap	57	Lake
20	Nose	58	Love
21	Note	59	Lap
22	Nun	60	Cheese
23	Name	61	Jet
24	Nero	62	Chain
25	Nail	63	Jam
26	Niche	64	Chair
27	Neck	65	Jelly
28	Navy	66	Church (or Judge)
29	Nap	67	Cheque
30	Mace	68	Chaff
31	Mat	69	Chap
32	Men	70	Case
33	Mama	71	Cat
34	Mare	72	Can
35	Mall	73	Cam
36	Mesh	74	Car
37	Mac	75	Goal
38	Mafia	76	Cage
39	Map	77	Cake
40	Rose	78	Cave
41	Rite	79	Cap
42	Run	80	Face
43	Ram	81	Fat
44	Rear	82	Fan
45	Rail	83	Foam
46	Rash	84	Fir
47	Rake	85	Veil
48	Rave	86	Fudge

87	Folk	94	Bar
88	Viva	95	Ball
89	Fop	96	Batch
90	Boss	97	Back
91	Bat	98	Pouffe
92	Bin	99	Pope
93	Bomb	100	Deuces

* A sailing command – see page 100.

I once knew a clever and learned man, with a high I.Q., who could do logarithmic tables in his head. When I explained to him how the "t-for-1" code enabled me to read numbers as words, so making them easy to remember, he seemed slow to understand. I went over it again. He shook his head. Surely, I thought, he cannot fail to comprehend something so logical. Why was he so slow? "But," he said, "why do you need to encode these numbers? They're perfectly memorable to me. Numbers are my friends. They have family relationships and values which would be lost if I dressed them up in disguises as you suggest." How humbling. It was me that was not being very bright.

Those of you with that kind of flair for figures may not need to translate figures into words. But, I tell you, when I was learning the Port-of-London Byelaws for my river police Sergeant's examination, I was able to grasp all the definitions and could tell you the section numbers of specific offences. This was very handy when confronting the argumentative master of a ship who was versed in merchant shipping law. The 't-for-1' code made it possible.

There are many like me who will never know the "language" of mathematics, and who are discouraged by the sight of numbers in an otherwise straightforward text. For those of us who are somewhat innumerate, therefore, the 't-for-1' code remains a useful contrivance. That is why someone took the trouble to devise it and why it has lasted so long.

Personal Identification Numbers (P.I.N.)

An obvious use for the 't-for-1' code is to remember P.I.N. (for bank automatic cashpoints), brief-case or other combination lock numbers, and computer access codes. We are advised never to write these numbers in a diary or anywhere else, but you may with greater security record a codeword or sentence based upon them.

Incidentally, a colleague who is a linguist showed me the diary note of his cashpoint P.I.N. It was in Arabic script. "No use knocking me down and mugging me for a translation", he laughed. "The words are Bulgarian." He has the right idea. To help your memory, always use what you know best.

Road Signs

I am not keen on driving a car although I do a fair amount of it. I resent particularly, being strapped and trapped behind the wheel for hours on end, not able to do much else but concentrate on the process of driving. My notion of luxury is a chauffeur who would whisk me around, freeing me to read, doze, watch the scenery or pursue a train of thought uninterrupted.

So, when I drove from my home at Tonbridge in the county of Kent, up North to the remote town of Hawes in North Yorkshire a little while ago, the car laden with equipment and exhibits for a residential lecture weekend, I wished more than once beforehand – and during the long journey – that I could afford someone to take the driving off my hands.

Map-reading, however, I enjoy; but, once on the way, I do not want to stop and look up turn-offs, road numbers, etc. Since I became a victim of middle-aged long-sightedness, it means hauling out my reading glasses, then remembering to take them off again prior to pulling out once more into traffic. As I often wear sun glasses, or night glasses, they too can be a complication – more impedimenta. Consequently, I prefer to memorise junctions along my route before setting off. (It occurs to me that this is also a contribution to road safety, since I am less likely to overshoot the turn-off I need, and then be tempted to stand on the brakes, execute a U-turn, or reverse to regain my route.)

Road numbers turn into many memorable words when the 't-for-1' code is applied to them. My trip from Tonbridge to Hawes went via Oakham, Rutland (for a nostalgic stopover at my birthplace). The first part was a familiar route around the M25 anti-clockwise to go off North at junction 23 along the A1(M) & (T).

The rest was new ground to me.

A606 . . . A6006 . . . A6(T) . . . M1 . . .A1(T) . . . A684

I wanted to fix these final 6 road numbers in my mind for the duration of the drive. No need to remember the 'A' or 'M' prefixes, nor the 'T' suffixes in brackets. I just needed the numbers, especially the 684 that was my turn-off after driving North for several hours onto the final leg West into Wensleydale. Taking into account my petty obsession with having a chauffeur, I was able to assemble the (admittedly ungrammatical) sentence:-

---

"I wiSH I haS the waGe whiCH
eaSe SuCH CHore To T' CHauFFeuR."

The capital letters represented the route numbers. Be clear, this seemingly convoluted way of storing away a few simple numbers is, with practice, easily done. It takes me longer here to explain it than it took to realise the sentence. Its very oddness made it memorable and it did the job.

Notice how I introduced several vowels and consonants that, in making the sentence, left the encoded numbers unchanged. Neither 'w' nor 'wh' count, so I could use the words "wish", "wage" and "which". 'H' has no value, making "has" still represent just '0'. The vowels 'ea' together ("ease") are otherwise valueless. "Chore" relied upon me choosing to ignore the possibility that 'r' might read '4', assuming instead that phonetically "chore" is "chaw".

Everyone who does so, uses and slightly abuses the 't-for-1' code until it becomes a very personal tool. Even fluent users may momentarily struggle to decipher and understand what another practitioner is up to. It is all right as long at it works for you.

The abbreviation of "the" to "t" is most apt, coming as it does just before "chauffeur" (the A684 into Wensleydale). It reminds me, like Yorkshire dialect written down, that I am at the Yorkshire turn-off.

Party Trick

Here is a way to demonstrate how good a trained memory can be. It takes about a quarter of an hour and your audience – who could be one solitary person, or a roomful – will always be entertained and impressed. I used to do this as one of a police boat crew, to while away a bit of time afloat on night duty on the Thames tideway.

Master strong mental images for keywords 1 to 20 inclusive. Ask your audience to give you, one at a time, 20 objects to remember. Link each one to its corresponding number in the order they are memorised. Your helpers can pick simple and mundane items (table, pen, light bulb) or complicated things (a mahogany tallboy with a damaged brass whatnot). It will make no difference. Do not deliberately hurry the memory process, although you may find you need no more than 15–20 seconds an object. Some may be done as quick as a wink, with practice, or a bit of luck if the mental link happens to be an easy one. Only call for the next item when you have stored away the previous one. Resist the urge to back-track and see if you can recall earlier words.

An independent witness must write down the numbers 1 – 20, and, alongside each number, the objects in the order supplied to you. This will be the checklist afterwards.

When you reach the final object, pause and ask if anyone else has tried to memorise the list along with you. One or two may say they tried. Ask if they succeeded. They will admit they gave up early on. You now recite aloud the list of objects from first to last. Occasionally, when performing this trick, you may be stuck for one or two objects. (This will be when your mental link was poorly chosen.) Do not worry about it. Come back to it later, or ask the list-keeper to prompt you. You will not forget it again.

Then, confident that you know the list (reciting it was the first chance you had to check), surprise them by reciting it backwards.

Now, really amaze them. Ask for numbers between 1 and 20 to be called out at random. You respond with the right object every time, obviously without having to work through the list. Finally, have objects called out and you tell them the corresponding numbers.

What an impact that has: yet, after only a few hours playing around with the 't-for-1' code, you can do it.

LESSON 8
PLAYING CARDS

"I am sorry I have not learnt to play at cards. It is very useful in life . . ."

Dr. Samuel Johnson (1709–1784)

Stories are ruefully told, even by professional magicians, of having had a card selected from the pack by a member of the audience, various things done to complicate the final effect . . . and then, halfway through all the shenanigans prior to revealing or identifying the card in question, the performer realised to his dismay that he had forgotten what card it was anyway.

I am not an accomplished card player, indulging only occasionally in the simplest games. I do, however, perform card tricks and so need to locate and memorise cards. It helps to have a system and the 't-for-1' code is best. With it you can commit to memory the sequence of all or part of a deck of cards; and, by systematically keeping track by one means or another of what high or low cards have gone, you can harness the law of probabilities more favourably in card games that are part chance and part skill. Rare individuals may be able to do this instinctively. Lucky them. I find the 't-for-1' code indispensable. Here is my method; it has a codeword for each of the 52 cards.

As a conjuror I perform several mystifying effects with cards, relying upon a stacked (pre-arranged) pack or deck which I must first memorise completely. To do this I use a codeword for each playing card and then must mentally link or pair each card codeword with the keyword from the list already shown you (see page 87). Thus I am able to represent each card's position from 1 to 52 in the stacked deck.

Here are my words and links.

Number (or Spot) Cards – Keywords

Number or spot cards have keywords with the first letters telling you their suits. Clubs begin with hard 'C' (or, in one exceptional case, 'K'). Hearts keywords all begin with 'H'. Spades with 'S'. Diamonds with 'D'. The other consonant tells you the number or value of each card.

	SPADES			DIAMONDS
2	Sun		2	Dane
3	Sum		3	Dame
4	Sir		4	Deer
5	Sail		5	Dolly (waterman's slang for a bollard)
6	Sash		6	Dish
7	Sack		7	Deck
8	Safe		8	Diva (an operatic prima donna)
9	Soap		9	Dip
10	Suits		10	Dots

Aces and Court cards, unlike plain number (or spot) cards, can suggest mental pictures. There is no need for a second codeword for them, as they can be linked directly to one or other of the original keywords to decide their places in our pre-arranged pack of cards.

Aces – Keywords

CLUBS – I picture a licensed or registered drinking club, a smart one like those I saw patrolling a beat in the 1950s Mayfair, and knew during my time with West End Central's

CLUBS	
2	Cane
3	Comb
4	Car
5	Koala (bear)
6	Cash
7	Cake
8	Cave
9	Cup
10	Cats

HEARTS	
2	Hen
3	Ham
4	Hair
5	Hull
6	Hush
7	Hook
8	Hive
9	Hip
10	Hoots

vice squad. I see the front of the building with the NAME in neon lighting over the door. That is my keyword, "NAME" (decoding to the number 23). In stacking a deck of cards I always place the Ace of Clubs 23 down from the top.

HEARTS – As a boy I became fascinated with anatomy and physiology, how the human body is built and works. I once bought a heart from the local butcher's shop and set about dissecting it with an old razor blade. The cutting edge was soon blunt. It surprised me how tough the muscle fibres were. That heart was like a lump of TANned leather; hence my keyword for the Ace of Hearts is TAN and that card goes No. 12 in an arranged deck.

SPADES – There was an Ace of Spades café where the owner, a pleasant matronly woman (known to the lorry drivers as "Mum" or "Ma"), served tea and meals. So my keyword for the Ace of Spades is "MAMA" and that card is 33rd in my pack.

DIAMONDS – Diamonds are a sign of wealth. One group

associated with getting rich quickly is that shady lot the Mafia. My keyword for the Ace of Diamonds is MAFIA (the 38th card).

Ace of Clubs	NAME	23
Ace of Hearts	TAN	12
Ace of Spades	MAMA	33
Ace of Diamonds	MAFIA	38

These keywords spring to mind because of peculiar and very personal ideas based upon my own lifetime of experiences. You may, or may not, see the logic in the connections. Do not try to absorb them yourself. Rather, make up your own.

Court (or Picture) Cards – Keywords

JACKS or KNAVES	CLUBS	Inside my imaginary West End drinking club I picture the Knave as a gambler. A gambler, forever with his eye on making a fortune, might well be attracted by a treasure MAP. That is my keyword, No. 39.
	HEARTS	The Knave of Hearts is in my mind an unfaithful lover or else the man who breaks up a marriage. This often results in all concerned coming under the spotlight of unwanted publicity . . . a RAY (No. 4).
	SPADES	The Knave of Spades I portray as an old-fashioned 'navvy', one of those "navigators" who dug the canals through England in the

17–1800s. Any power used on the site was horsepower and I am told by those who know that mares worked best. So MARE is my codeword, No. 34.

DIAMONDS   The Knave of Diamonds is to me a thief. The Taro pack has 22 extra cards, one of which is 'The Hanged Man'. As you were once hanged for stealing I make TARO my keyword and place the Jack of Diamonds in 14th place in my arranged deck of cards.

QUEENS   CLUBS   Back yet again in my imaginary West End club, I see the Queen of Clubs as one of Howard Heffner's Bunny-girls. She is chewing a TOFFEE, my keyword (18).

HEARTS   The Queen of Hearts I see as the ultimate female lover. Reality falls short. In all love, real or prostituted, there is a price to be paid. FEE is the codeword – No. 8.

SPADES   When the men went off to fight in World War II, the women were drafted into factories or onto farms and did the work of the absent men. The farm girls were known as "landgirls". So my Queen of Spades is a landgirl, feeding a flock of sheep that includes a RAM, 43.

DIAMONDS   A glittering diamond tiara is

worn by Her Royal Highness the Princess Diana to social functions. Princess Di is very slender (or lightweight). Thus my keyword is LIGHT – 51.

KINGS	CLUBS	I mentioned earlier the picturesque May-time walk enjoyed by visitors and residents alike in my home town of Bournemouth. One would sometimes see, taking the air and looking prosperous in evening dress, an hotelier or club owner. The keyword for the King of Clubs (club owner) is MAY (3).
	HEARTS	My King of Hearts is a bridegroom. I once saw a hilarious sketch in an old music hall by a midget dressed as a bridegroom. So my keyword for the King of Hearts is TICH (16).
	SPADES	A gardener represents the King of Spades to me. I imagine him sitting in the garden shed, resting from his toil, and taking a tot of whisky. TOT (11)
	DIAMONDS	I suppose a jeweller handles the most precious stones and so qualifies to be known as the King of Diamonds. Jewellers are rarely seen without an eyeglass and a pair of pliers at the ready. The keyword is TOOL (15).

Deck Sequence

Once you can quickly think of the codeword for each

individual spot card, and the mental pictures for aces and
court cards, it only remains to pair them mentally with the
main keywords 1 to 52. Then you will have memorised a
stacked deck. This makes it possible to identify any card
chosen at random from the pack by a volunteer. All you need
do is sneak a peek at one or other of the two cards
immediately above or below the selected card. As you will
know its location, simply count one forward or backward
from it and name the card linked with the resulting keyword.
With some showmanship, many entertaining effects can be
done this way to baffle an audience.

To link any card with its position in the pack, make a
mental association between the keyword for that card and
the relevant keyword from 1 to 52 (see page 87). This is how
I prearrange and remember every card in a stacked deck.
(Abbreviations:- AD = Ace of Diamonds; 4S = Four of
Spades; 10H = Ten of Hearts; JC = Jack of Clubs; etc.)

1.	(Tea)	6D (Dish)	A great saucer-shaped dish full of steaming brown tea.
2.	(Noah)	5C (Koala)	Bearded biblical patriarch Noah, afloat in his Ark with all the animals of creation, holding a cuddly koala bear in his arms.
3.	(May)	KC (Club owner)	See page 99.
4.	(Ray)	JH (Co-respondant)	See page 97.
5.	("Lee-O")	5S (Sail)	"Lee-O" is a warning called out by the helmsman prior to changing tack in a sailing craft.
6.	(Shaw)	9D (Dip)	The late George Bernard

Shaw, Irish dramatist and writer, trousers rolled up, tentatively dipping his toes into the sea prior to a paddle.

7. (Key) 9S (Soap) Those keen on crime novels will know that one way to obtain an outline copy of a key is to press it into a piece of soap.

8. (Fee) QH (Lover) See page 98.

9. (Bay) 3C (Comb) A golf course bunker, like a sandy seaside bay, is combed with a large rake to smooth the sand.

10. (Toes) 10C (Cats) Cats, like many animals, actually walk on their toes. Their 4 small "feet" with claws and pads are actually just the leading parts of their whole feet. What looks like a knee bent the wrong way is the heel.

11. (Tot) KS (Gardener) See page 99.

12. (Tan) AH (Leather) See page 96.

13. (Team) 4D (Deer) A typical photograph of a football or cricket team, is assembled in rows. Above and behind them, grinning at the camera, is the mounted head of a deer hung on the wall as a trophy.

14. (Taro) JD (Thief) See page 98.

15. (Tool)   KD (Jeweller)   See page 99.

16. (Tich)   KH (Bride-
              groom)   See page 99.

17. ('tec)   2D (Dane)   A private detective tracks
                               his quarry with a dog, a
                               great Dane on a lead.

18. (Toffee) QC (Bunny-
              girl)   See page 98.

19. (Tap)   9C (Cup)   A drinking water tap with a
                               metal cup attached to it by
                               a chain.

20. (Nose)   10H (Hoots)   Someone noisily blowing
                               his nose so that it trumpets
                               or hoots.

21. (Note)   8D (Diva)   A diva sings notes.

22. (Nun)   2C (Cane)   Both are associated in
                               different ways with strict
                               discipline.

23. (Name)   AC (Club)   See page 95.

24. (Nero)   7H (Hook)   Nero is said to have fiddled
                               while Rome burned
                               (impossible, as the violin
                               had not then been
                               invented). The fingering
                               hand of a violinist is turned
                               and clawed like a hook.

25. (Nail)   7C (Cake)   A birthday cake skewered
                               to the table by an
                               enormous nail.

26. (Niche)   4S (Sir)   In the niches of some
                               churches are placed stone
                               figures of knights (Sirs).

27. (Neck)   7S   (Sack)   A sack is tied closed at the neck.

28. (Navy)   9H   (Hip)   A curvaceous bathing belle lies on her side on the beach, upper hip prominent. A convoy of tiny ships sails up and over the protruding hip-bone, as if on a lumpy sea.

29. (Nap)   8S   (Safe)   A safe door is open and inside is a vagrant fast asleep.

30. (Mace)   6S   (Sash)   A mace is a ceremonial staff carried as a symbol of authority. The mace-bearer is in uniform, wearing a sash.

31. (Mat)   6C   (Cash)   The 'Brinks-Mat' robbery was a major theft of cash.

32. (Men)   2H   (Hen)   A simple rhyme. A lot of men with a hen.

33. (Mama)   AS   (Cafe)   See page 96.

34. (Mare)   JS   (Navvy)   See page 97.

35. (Mall)   4C   (Car)   The Mall is the London thoroughfare leading from Admiralty Arch to Buckingham Palace, with cars flowing along it.

36. (Mesh)   5H   (Hull)   A fishing trawler lies hove-to while the net is hauled aboard.

37. (Mac)   10S   (Suits)   A raincoat is worn over a suit.

38. (Mafia)	AD (Dia-monds)	See page 96.
39. (Map)	JC (Gambler)	See page 97.
40. (Rose)	4H (Hair)	A rose may be worn in the hair.
41. (Rite)	2S (Sun)	Some cultures worshipped the sun by performing religious rites.
42. (Run)	7D (Deck)	On ocean-going passenger liners it was usual to measure out a course around the deck so that passengers could run or walk for exercise.
43. (Ram)	QS (Landgirl)	See page 98.
44. (Rear)	3H (Ham)	'Hams' is an informal term for the buttocks or the rear of the thighs.
45. (Rail)	3S (Sum)	A white-painted handrail upon which, amidst the graffiti, someone has scratched a sum.
46. (Rash)	8C (Cave)	A cave entrance, covered in clusters of sea anemones (like a rash).
47. (Rake)	10D (Dots)	A rake banged down on soil makes lots of dots with its pointed tines.
48. (Rave)	6H (Hush)	"Hush" might soothe a raving person.
49. (Rope)	5D (Dolly)	"Dolly" is waterman's slang for a bollard, over

			which mooring ropes are placed.
50.	(Lace)	3D (Dame)	Lace-making is an activity for an elderly lady (or dame).
51.	(Light)	QD (Princess Di)	See page 98.
52.	(Lane)	8H (Hive)	A country lane with beehives beside it.

Make Your Own List

Once again I stress mental associations are personal things. An odd, ludicrous or striking notion of your own is far better than one of mine. My list shows how I do it. If any one of them strikes a chord – fine – use it. Otherwise, sit down with paper and pencil and devise your own. By the time you have worked out suitable links, you will not have to learn them. Concentrating upon them will have been work enough to fix them firmly in your mind. Make sure you rehearse them from time to time until they are reinforced for good.

LESSON 9
STUDY FOR EXAMS

"Examinations are formidable even to the best prepared, for the greatest fool may ask more than the wisest man can answer."

Charles COLTON (1780–1832)

You have decided to study for some examination or other. Are you resigned to becoming a hermit – to long hours spent in solitary confinement, text books open, with no distractions? Have you briefed your spouse, family and friends to leave you undisturbed? If so, you are misguided. That is probably the least effective method of study known.

You know for sure, before you start, that after 5 minutes you will be bored. After 10 minutes your eyelids will droop and, even if you fight the feeling, you will read and re-read the same paragraph and still not absorb it. After a quarter of an hour the clock will appear to have stopped – and you will be finding excuses to do so too.

Make It Easy

Acquiring knowledge can, for those who know how to go about it, be fun. It is a game that is never tiresome, to which we return again and again, where the hours pass unnoticed and we are so involved that only pointed remarks from others drag us reluctantly out of it. And there ARE ways – believe me – to make it so. Follow my advice and study cannot be tedious. Adopt my ideas and you must enlarge your learning power. Let me convince you.

First, abandon the silly notion that study has to be an unpleasant chore. Clever people are not any brighter than you or I, nor do they work any harder to acquire their knowledge. They may actually spend less time studying but they use it well. Time management entails knowing the difference between being 'efficient' and 'effective'. The world is full of efficient souls who do their absolute best at all they attempt. Sadly, they are often not very successful, sometimes being downright second-rate. Efficiency is "doing things right", whereas 'effectiveness' is "doing the right things". Be selective. Confine your efforts to what will further your aims and objectives. Clever people may even make a game of study. Certainly they recall better because they store facts and figures away sensibly where they can be readily retrieved. Well, you know how to do that now.

"Aha" Experiences

Much so-called intelligence is really just good memory. Creative individuals are quick to recognise patterns and connections. "Aha, yes. I see. Of course. Got it." When you say that, you are recalling a number of known facts and marshalling them into an order that suddenly sheds light on something you did not previously understand. That fresh concept can then be memorised and recollected when needed. It is an "Aha" experience. Aim to have more "Aha" experiences. They are good for your confidence and self-esteem. Improve your memory and you will feel cleverer too.

Use Your 5 Senses

We all, when free from handicap, sample the world around us via our 5 senses:-

1. HEARING,
2. SIGHT,
3. TOUCH,
4. SMELL,
5. TASTE.

Realise that you learn better when you bring more than one of these senses to bear on the matter in hand. Mostly we rely upon only the single sense of hearing when people lecture us, or solely sight when we read for ourselves. Even when the book is gripping, or the speaker has a flair for bringing his topic to life, it is an ineffective way to learn. That is why classrooms are equipped with blackboards or overhead projectors and film screens, so that you can be shown drawings and pictures, to involve a second sense (sight). Still, most classroom work is necessarily limited to talk and chalk.

The best teachers and lecturers, tutors and coaches, will contrive to have students indulge in practical sessions whenever possible, bringing into play your senses of touch, smell and taste, for example by doing experiments with chemistry, carpentry or cooking. Always use as many senses as you can to memorise an important idea.

Psychologists tell us smells make the most indelible memories. A smell can bring long-gone circumstances flooding back in detail after a lapse of years. It is therefore a pity that this particular sense cannot often be used in private study or the classroom. Students should try to poke their noses in more often.

A lecturer was stressing to his students how the pursuit of knowledge required them at all times to be observant. He produced a bowl of coloured liquid and proceeded to demonstrate how to utilise all 5 senses. He held it up to the light and observed its colour; listened to how it splashed; sniffed it; and finally dipped his finger into it and tasted it. Then he passed the container around the class for each student to do the same. As they tasted it they screwed up their faces and exclaimed in disgust. It was foul. Afterwards the lecturer said; "Now, ladies and gentlemen, that was a useful lesson in using all your senses upon an object of interest. I expect you will remember this experiment. By the way, how many of you noticed that the finger I dipped into the liquid was NOT the finger that I put in my mouth?"

Choosing Books

What do you want to learn? Gardening? Cookery? A foreign language? How to pass the driving test? Chess?

Making a speech? Keeping pets? Letter writing? Selling your house? How to slim? Telling jokes? Do not buy or borrow books just because they are included in someone's list of recommended reading. What is a helpful book for me might be useless to you. I once worked with a sociology graduate who claimed he had never owned or read a book in his life. It was not literally true, of course. He was making the point that students should dip selectively into textbooks (not try to read them from cover to cover like novels), and, as most are quite costly, they should be borrowed from a free lending library. Only if you find yourself repeatedly borrowing a particular book because you find it indispensable, might you then consider buying that one.

Of course, at school or college, the required reading may have to come from set textbooks. In that case you have no choice, but you should still try to supplement them with other source material.

There is a way to work out if a book is right for you. First find an abundant source of books on your chosen subject. Look in the front at the date of publication or of its most recent revised edition. If it is 1970-something-or-other, generally speaking, put it back on the shelf. Life is changing so fast it may well be out-of-date. There are exceptions, and you need to appreciate that writings about some subjects become out-of-date much less quickly than others. For example, an old book on public speaking may be a gem unsurpassed by subsequent authorship, whereas a tome about computing may be hopelessly out of touch within a few short months. Equally, the researcher of any sort of history will glean lots of background material from old treatises. However, for many subjects, whilst a 1980's book might be okay, a 1990's one is preferable.

Next look in the alphabetical index at the back of the book for any references to what you want to know. Turn them up. Are they obviously readable? Are there perhaps, clear diagrams? If so, that is the book for you. If not, leave it. Try another.

Any book you do not fancy at once, put it back on the

shelf. Do not bother with it. Life is too short; your time and energy are too valuable to waste trying to make sense of complicated or obscure texts. That is the author's job. If the print is too small, if there are algebraic formulae you will never understand, if every page has scholarly footnotes and cross-references, forget it. Unless – of course – you are the bright academic sort who revels in that kind of thing. In that case, keep the book and discard this one.

A handy word for us students is "windmill". Every time you meet a word or sentence you do not understand in a textbook, say "windmill" instead and pass on. Often further reading will make clear the earlier hard bit. When it does not, it may not be vital anyway. But – be warned – when too many "windmills" crop up in each page, that is the wrong book for you. Put it back. Choose only books with very few "windmills".

I hope that by now you have got clear in your mind that study should be easy . . . so stop trying to make it hard.

Using Books

Always read 2 or 3 books on the same subject. Then you will be told the same things in slightly different ways by the different authors. This will make the facts clearer and reinforce them. Information that features in all the books can safely be assumed to be fundamental and worth noting. Where writers differ on some point, there is room for personal opinion.

I repeat, do not try to read textbooks. They are not stories but works of reference and study. Look up just the bit you need. Sort it out and stow the data away in that mental wardrobe of yours where you can find it again later. Then shut the book. Soaking up knowledge a bit at a time this way is fairly effortless, so there is no need to shut yourself away. Watch T.V. Play with the children. Have friends and neighbours in and make conversation with them. Keep the book handy, however, because you might want to dip into it again before the day is over to find out the answer to some other question that pops into your head. And you can do that while carrying on a normal existence.

One advantage of owning textbooks is that you can write in them. I know it was impressed upon us as children that we should not deface books. That was then, when we lacked discretion. This is now. Most practised students ring around, underline, or otherwise highlight significant bits of text with a coloured pen. So, deciding what books to buy should form a part of your study plan.

Notice how each paragraph in a book often has only one crucial sentence. All the rest is padding, enlarging upon the original idea and giving examples. Underline that single sentence. Do it for the entire chapter; eventually throughout the whole book. The sentences so highlighted should, by themselves, form a continuous narrative and make sense. When you come to revise, READ ONLY THE UNDER-LINED PARTS. The complete book can thus be scanned in 10–15 minutes. You will discover, though, that the concentration you devoted to deciding which words should be underlined and which omitted from that treatment, has also given you a sound grasp of the remainder of the contents. This is because you employed the 6 guiding principles rather than just tried to memorise the text.

Rote Learning – Right or Wrong?

Learning "by rote" means memorising by means of repetition with little or no attempt at understanding, e.g. chanting multiplication tables, reciting poetry or proverbs or formulae. It is viewed with disfavour by educationalists because lack of thought implies lack of comprehension. At its worst, it could be brainwashing, with pupils conditioned into unquestioning acceptance of facts that are misleading or downright wrong, but which have become ingrained by repetition. Tests and examinations that rely too much upon mere recall (facts, not thinking) are also condemned. Students, it is argued, can be overawed and overwhelmed by the amount to be absorbed and may as a consequence actually learn less. Rote learning has become greatly discredited and there has grown up a feeling in some circles that word perfect learning is always wrong, somehow indecent, and many tutors and students shy away from it.

I believe that is wrong. Do not reject word perfect learning altogether. Teachers rightly place greater emphasis upon the so-called "higher" skills, such as a search for meaning and understanding, critical faculties, the capacity for reasoned argument, creativity, logic and problem-solving. Fair enough. These higher skills depend, however, upon a great deal of memorised facts stored away and awaiting recall. It is invaluable to be able to think "on your feet" in academic debate, sports contest, theatrical performance, industrial negotiations, parlour games, or a court of law. Those who do it best are those who can recall pertinent facts at will.

During 25 years in the Metropolitan Police, a big city cop (and proud of it), I had to meet all sorts of challenges, from facing down some villain who might attack me, to resisting the tactics in Court of an astute defence lawyer. It was not possible to carry around all the books I might need. Legal powers, duties, telling arguments, had to be kept in my head. Knowledge was all I had. I was once doing undercover work in a back street drinking den and looked up to find myself facing a man I had earlier put in prison. It was his first evening of freedom having served his sentence. He had gone for a drink and come face-to-face with me. Talk yourself out of that. I had to; and it was a confrontation I had to win.

Some word perfect learning was also essential to me when I was a manager of swimming pools and leisure centres, e.g. emergency procedures and contingency plans. I would have been an inept fool if I had had to retire to my office to read up what to do in the event of a gas escape in the plant room, or a bomb threat received by phone. I had to have the written procedures and codes of practice firmly implanted in my mind, ready for prompt recall even if they were needed only very infrequently. so they had to be learnt word perfect.

On the other hand, I had no need to commit to memory the Council's discipline and grievance procedures. They could be read and a course of action decided without the delay being harmful.

Homework

Put together answers to set homework questions with the aid of open text-books and written notes. Take as long as you need. Spread the task over several days, if needs be. Do not limit yourself to doing them under strict examination conditions.

Tutors are not always keen on this way of working. They tend to point out that you are fooling yourself as to your real ability; that you are gaining high marks unfairly; that you will not be able to reproduce the same high standard in an exam . . . that you are close to cheating. They prefer to mark an effort done without any assistance and in the bare time allowed.

Well, trial and error is one way to learn. Trial without all that error is better.

Compiling homework answers under exam conditions can only lead to half-baked results, attracting poor marks and a lot of red ink corrections. This is supposed to be part of the learning process; but practise mediocre standards (as you must by this system) and you will be second-rate on examination day.

Concentrate instead on preparing a comprehensive and well-presented answer. Collect, collate and edit all relevant data. The effort will teach you much more. Also, when you come to revise, you will be reading first-class notes. By using the 6 guiding principles, while working on homework, you will remember a lot more too.

Will you be able to do it on exam day? Yes, you will. For a start you will know far more about each topic than you can possibly put down. You will have to be choosy about what you write. Contrast your enviable condition with that of the average candidate who is struggling to dredge up enough decent material to be sure of a pass mark. You will not need to pad, but, in ruthlessly eliminating material, you will produce a rich distilled essence of all you know: and, under pressure and charged with excitement, you will write more – much more – than you could during a routine bit of classwork. Believe me, even on a bad day with an unfortunate exam paper, you will still be very, very good indeed.

Aim for the stars. Then, although you go off course and miss, you will end up very high.

Whether you attend a college or undertake a correspondence course, do the homework. It is essential. What you rehearse in your homework is what you will eventually produce in examinations.

Examinations, despite the best efforts of examining bodies, are nothing to do with real life and work. So do not delude yourself that because you are employed a certain way, or pursue a leisure interest expertly, that you can cope with test questions without first studying what is required of you. Absorb all the theory you will need; then use homework to practise airing that knowledge. Swap tit-bits for marks from examiners.

Create a style of writing and page layout that will be an unthinking habit by the day of the exam. Use only one pen (blue or black) for most of your writing, with another of a different colour for headings, underlining, etc. These two, along with a straight edge rule, will also do for drawings. (Pencils are out of favour these days.)

Memorise all diagrams you are likely to have to reproduce, so that you can dash them off without thought as quickly as possible. Answers to some questions can be anticipated, prepared and practised beforehand. Certainly commit to memory opening paragraphs that will serve to get you started on an answer or two. These are extra instances where rote learning (discussed earlier) can be justified. It saves sucking your pen and gazing at the ceiling for inspiration. Once you start writing, then your mind will move on ahead to keep you going.

Must Knows, Should Knows & Could Knows

Mentally label everything you must learn as one of 3 categories:-

1. MUST KNOWS,
2. SHOULD KNOWS, and
3. COULD KNOWS.

'Must Knows' are indispensable. You cannot hope for a pass mark unless they are included. Then aim to pick up more marks by adding 'Should Knows'. 'Could Knows' are little extras (perhaps quoting the source of a reference and some details of the author). They can turn a good pass into an excellent one – but do not spend time on them until you have satisfied the examiner with enough of categories 1 & 2. Focusing your mind on what goes into which category uses the 6 guiding principles and so aids effortless learning.

Learn, from past exam papers and specimen answers (where available) what examiners seek and give it to them. Demonstrate originality based upon experience, if you can, but do not be unorthodox. Examiners are prudent souls. Your exam paper is most definitely NOT the place to try out some idea that is not already known to the person who will mark it.

Collect and study exam papers for the past 3–4 years. As a general rule do not go back any further. Examiners' requirements change with time. Do every single question for homework. It is not cheating, nor is it a lazy short-cut. Rather, it is a way to get you interested and involved over a length of time. It gives you a study syllabus framework. Some of the questions may come up in a future exam paper. The topics will certainly recur worded another way. Do not be tempted to make up a short-list of fancied questions you hope will appear, limiting study to these only, as it does not work. Do, however, note the way previous questions are worded and the frequency with which certain topics crop up. Then your mind will be alert to spot 'Must Knows' and 'Should Knows', extract them from study material, and file them securely in your long-term memory.

LESSON 10
CONCLUSIONS

"A memory is what is left behind when something happens and does not completely unhappen . . . curry stains on the table cloth are an example."

Edward de Bono (1969)

Review of the 6 'Guiding Principles'.

1. MINUTES, not seconds

Learning anything takes a little time. A littered room can be comically tidied by playing a film backwards, so that everything flies magically into place in a few seconds. It is, however, too quick and fleeting to remember. You must allow time for new ideas to sink in; and be prepared to go slower with hard stuff.

Most of us can think of a time when a problem had us beaten. After much stewing and fretting we finally gave up. That night, or perhaps days later, the answer came to us "out of the blue". Take note. What happened was that your brain went on working out the problem, without you being aware of it, and only alerted you when it had something to report. What an ally. Understand that you must do the work first. Absorb the data. Make an effort to sort it out and understand it. Attempt solutions to problems. Once you have done all that conscientiously – and NOT before – it is a reliable technique to give up. Put it to the back of your mind. Leave your subconscious free to have a go for you. Provided you have given it enough to go on, it will surprise you how clever it (you) can be.

2. EVALUATE

Do take careful stock of your task. Do not just turn up for your first lesson of a course, or open correspondence notes at page 1, and trust that it will somehow make sense as the weeks go by. It will not. Scan the entire syllabus. Break it up and rearrange it to suit you wherever you can. Bring forward topics you find simple and get them out of the way. Find out how much hard stuff there is. That will require a special effort later, and time must be allowed for it.

It is not always possible to look ahead or to re-structure the syllabus when you are a young person at school or college, whereas adults at an evening institute often can persuade instructors to vary course material to suit their needs. There is a way around the problem. To obtain sneak previews of forthcoming work without being awkward or upsetting tutors, persuade scholars and students who are further advanced than you to show you their notes and handouts, and discuss the material with them.

Read ahead. Find out what your teacher has planned for later and familiarise yourself with it now. You can understand and enjoy the subtle bits in a complicated spy thriller or murder mystery better when you have already seen the film or read the book before. You know how it ends and so can concentrate more on how the clues connect within the plot. It is the same with a course of instruction.

Tutors may not be keen on you skipping about in their rigid timetable which progresses step-by-step in a way they consider best suited to your needs. Of course there must be an overall plan, but too strict an adherence to the calendar takes no account of the fact that you are human. You learn better in fits and starts. When you are enjoying yourself and making progress, keep at it. When the mood disappears, you are sick or on holiday, give it a rest with a clear conscience. You know from looking ahead and taking stock of the task when a renewed sense of urgency is needed. Then you can return refreshed to study again.

When I was new to the leisure industry, I had to learn about poolwater treatment and also the chemistry of laundry work. They have a lot in common. It made sense to learn them together and that is what I did. In my study course they were separated and not even in the same term. Take careful stock and then arrange your own personal approach to study and memory work.

3. MAKE AN EFFORT

Learning or remembering must be done by the learner. It is not some sort of transmission process that emanates from the tutor; nor do you absorb it through the pores by simply carrying lots of the right books around with you. Many students consider, at one time or another, dictating study material into a tape recorder so that they can listen to it whilst driving the car or prior to going to sleep at night. A few claim it works. Umm. I doubt it works well. It is too passive. Learning is an active process. You must involve yourself more than that. You remembered all the items in the rearranged wardrobe (see page 10) because you did it yourself. It would not have worked if you had merely watched someone else do it for you, or even if you had acted under their directions.

The best trick I know for getting to grips with strange new material is to pretend I must teach it to someone that very next day. (Let's face it, as a college lecturer, that is a real and continual preoccupation; but, even when it is not, I can sharpen my wits noticeably by pretending to myself it is.) That way I must concentrate hard and ask myself; "What does this mean?" "What are the main points?" How can I simplify it?" "Is there a code word to make it memorable?" Finding the answers, I quickly master it myself.

4. ORDER THE DATA

Re-stocking that wardrobe, you put everything where it made sense, either in its own space or with some other thing you saw as allied to it. Memorise things the same way. Almost all you learn can be linked to something else you already know. Very rarely you might have to file a topic away in your head labelled "new & strange". The sooner you link another idea with it, the more certain you can be of retrieving both again.

When I tell a class something they did not know before (e.g. "Water alone is not a good wetting agent." True. That is why soap or a detergent is added), it sometimes makes them squirm in their seats and shuffle their feet. I have contradicted what they thought they knew and they grow uneasy. Gaining knowledge is often an uncomfortable experience. Try to have your peace of mind disturbed more often. "Whoa. Wait a second. Let's get this straight!" is something you ought to say a lot. Upset your cosy notions with a new fact or two. Then restore calm to your troubled brain by sorting out the strange idea that has intruded. Once it makes sense, you learn. And a mind stretched by a new idea never returns to its old dimensions.

5.   REINFORCE

Swots bore lesser mortals by airing their knowledge; but they are not showing off (well, not simply showing off). They are more likely reassuring themselves that they can still recall it. By talking about what they know, they reinforce it. They like an audience to help them remember, anyone who can be made to listen. Someone who knows enough to question, discuss, and occasionally correct them, is better. So the best place of all is in class. Try it yourself. Quiz teachers. Contribute to discussions. It really works. Newly acquired knowledge, especially, must not be left alone. Review it.

6.   CURIOSITY

Tell me you do not like a subject and I suspect at once that you do not understand it. If you do not understand it, how can you like it? Once you can understand it, it will intrigue you. Then you will learn.

An area that is a mystery to you is where you will learn most. Welcome it as a field in your study programme where there is most scope for remarkable improvement. Viewed this way, some of the dislike must surely yield to cautious curiosity. Then it becomes possible to marshall some enthusiasm to attack it. Great self confidence comes when you master a skill – theoretical or physical – which you had always assumed was beyond you. As a young lad I was unathletic and useless at ball games. In my 40s I trained to swim 5–10 miles in cold open waters and taught myself to Eskimo-roll a kayak. Aged 52 I could juggle and ride a unicycle. I walk tall with satisfaction at these achievements. I do not mean to boast. It does not matter to me that nobody I pass in the street is aware of what I can do. I know . . . and it makes me feel better. You can enjoy that feeling too.

Party Games

1. KIM'S GAME

I was introduced to this mental exercise in the 1940s when it was a traditional part of all Boy Scout observation training; and we also played it in neighbours' houses at parties where we entertained ourselves. It was called 'The Jewel Game' by Rudyard Kipling, the Indian-born British poet and novelist, in his book *Kim* (published in 1901).

Kim was a poor white lad, "burned black as any native", who was taught something of a lesson by a younger, 10-year-old Hindu boy who bested him at identifying a handful of precious and semi-precious stones on a copper tray. These were studied by both boys, then covered with an old newspaper. Kim recalled well but the smaller child not only knew the types of stones; he knew their flaws, whether or not they were drilled for a necklace, their weights, and so on as well. He even offered to do it blindfold, merely feeling the stones, and still excelled. Later they competed with other odds and ends from the shop, piles of swords or daggers, photos of natives, etc.

So, strictly speaking, Kim's Game should be played with a batch of similar objects. In fact assorted items, no two alike, are usually placed upon the tray and covered with a cloth. When the cloth is removed, all present have a short-ish time to commit to memory (no note-taking allowed) as many items as they can. The tray is then re-covered and removed, whereupon they must write down all they can recall. Twenty objects and about 2 minutes is about right, ensuring a reasonable rate of recall but separating the quick from the slow.

Performance improves with practice. Teach someone the months-of-the-year trick (see page 30), give them 12 objects, and they will score full marks. The 't-for-1' code (see page 82) will cope with any number. Do not let your eyes rove aimlessly over the tray's contents but rather, focus on each in turn so as to impose a numerical sequence upon them. Take care to divide the time available by the number of objects and strictly ration the attention you give to each one.

2. KIM'S GAME (variant)

Display only 10 objects. Competitors must memorise them in a short time. After removal, the order is rearranged. Players look again and have to identify which bits and pieces have been moved.

3. WITNESS

This is a chance to indulge in amateur dramatics. A few of your party are briefed to act out a scene for the others, who must afterwards write down what they saw. The witnesses may be warned beforehand what will occur; or, alternatively, the action can be sprung on them unexpectedly. It is surprising how widely people's perceptions of an event can vary.

4. CHESS MASTER

Set up a chess or draughts board with a layout of a few pawns and pieces. Players are given a period of time to study the arrangement, which is then removed or covered. They must reproduce the pattern on squared paper or another board.

5. PICTURE PARADE

Prepare by cutting out attractive coloured pictures from magazines and similar sources, pasting them onto thick paper or thin card sheets. Number them 1 to 20. Display them one at a time for as little as 5 seconds each. Players try to recall who or what they saw, in the correct order or simply anyhow. Keep to simple pictures, e.g. a tree, a yacht, a house, etc. Complicated ones (say, a street scene) will only puzzle because nobody knows what to look at. People will have little or no trouble recalling well-known faces (Her Majesty the Queen) or landmarks (Tower Bridge) but falter over anonymous people and objects.

6.   IDENTIFICATION PARADE
Players look at a group of people milling around. They look again and one or two have gone. Who has disappeared?

7.   FASHION PARADE
Look at one person for ½-a-minute. Then, when that person has left the room, describe in detail what he or she was wearing.

8.   PELMANISM
Shuffle a pack of cards and lay them face down upon a table. Players (usually just 2) take it in turns to turn up a pair of cards of their choice. When they happen upon two of a kind, the pair is withdrawn from play and kept by the successful player. Dissimilar pairs are turned face down again but kept in exactly the same place. As play continues, it becomes possible to remember where certain cards are located, increasing the chance of making a pair. The game ends when all the cards have been claimed and the winner is, of course, the one with the most pairs completed.

9.   COLOUR CODES
About 6 people are lined up and assigned a colour each, which is laid at their feet. The line is rearranged. Players have to identify each person by his original colour.

10.   SHOPPING
This is one of the many games in which the repetition of an

ever growing accumulation of nonsense words and/or actions is demanded of the players, until in turn each one fails and is eliminated. My wife played this one recently at a local branch of the Women's Institute.

Starting with the statement; "I went to the supermarket yesterday and bought . . ." players take it in turn to repeat the words, each adding a commodity, thus:-

1st person; "I went to the supermarket yesterday and bought . . . an orange."

2nd person; "I went to the supermarket yesterday and bought . . . an orange, and a packet of crisps."

3rd person; "I went . . . . . . and bought an orange, a packet of crisps and a large cauliflower."

4th person; "I . . . . . an orange, a packet of crisps, a large cauliflower, and a box of kippers."

USEFUL JARGON

ACRONYM A word made from the initial letters of words in a phrase or title; e.g. S.A.L.T. (Strategic Arms Limitation Talks).

ANAGRAM A word or phrase created by rearranging the letters of another word or phrase; e.g. live, vile, evil & veil.

BRAIN That part of the central nervous system housed within the skull, concerned with a variety of functions including memory.

INTELLIGENCE Thinking and reasoning power based upon acquired knowledge.

LEARNING Knowing through study or experience; often meaning to memorise (e.g. "learning a speech").

MEMORY Mental storage and retrieval or recall of past experience. When linked with subconscious physical response, the result is a learned reaction.

MIND A comprehensive name for many conscious and unconscious processes, including memory ("to bring to mind").

MNEMONIC A memory aid, such as an 'Anagram' or 'Acronym'.

PELMANISM A proprietary name (The Pelman Institute, London) now generally associated with any form of systematic memory training.

RECALL   Remembering stimulated by association of ideas.

RECOLLECTION   Bringing together once more ideas distributed or dissipated (to recollect one's calm or control). In memory terms, it seems to imply remembering plus a degree of effort or determination to succeed in remembering.

REMEMBERING   Memory working easily, thinking once more of something retained in the mind ("Ah yes. I remember it well.")

THE KNOT BOOK

Learn how to apply the right knot – secure and strong enough for the job. Such skill is not only immensely satisfying, but can be essential to the safety and enjoyment of leisure pursuits such as climbing, sailing and fishing; in rescue, life can depend on it.

Geoffrey Budworth has selected more than 100 knots spanning over 30 years' practical knotting – from young Sea Scout to knotting consultant: he advises the National Maritime Museum, Greenwich, is a founder member of the International Guild of Knot-Tyers and created the knot identification method used by police forensic scientists.

TEACH YOUR CHILD TO SWIM PROPERLY

Geoffrey Budworth shows how parents *can* teach their children to swim. Starting with the toddler or even baby, mum or dad can provide all the help and training needed.

The author is a highly qualified and experienced swimming teacher and coach, as well as being an accomplished long-distance open-water swimmer.

RIGHT WAY
PUBLISHING POLICY

HOW WE SELECT TITLES

RIGHT WAY consider carefully every deserving manuscript. Where an author is an authority on his subject but an inexperienced writer, we provide first-class editorial help. The standards we set make sure that every **RIGHT WAY** book is practical, easy to understand, concise, informative and delightful to read. Our specialist artists are skilled at creating simple illustrations which augment the text wherever necessary.

CONSISTENT QUALITY

At every reprint our books are updated where appropriate, giving our authors the opportunity to include new information.

FAST DELIVERY

We sell **RIGHT WAY** books to the best bookshops throughout the world. It may be that your bookseller has run out of stock of a particular title. If so, he can order more from us at any time – we have a fine reputation for "same day" despatch, and we supply any order, however small (even a single copy), to any bookseller who has an account with us. We prefer you to buy from your bookseller, as this reminds him of the strong underlying public demand for **RIGHT WAY** books. Readers who live in remote places, or who are housebound, or whose local bookseller is unco-operative, can order direct from us by post.

FREE

If you would like an up-to-date list of all **RIGHT WAY** titles currently available, please send a stamped self-addressed envelope to

ELLIOT RIGHT WAY BOOKS,
KINGSWOOD, SURREY, KT20 6TD, U.K.